Women Sex Offenders

Adele Mayer

Lp Learning Publications, Inc.
HOLMES BEACH, FL

ISBN: 1-55691-063-0

© 1992 by Adele Mayer

Learning Publications, Inc.
5351 Gulf Drive
P.O. Box 1338
Holmes Beach, FL 34218

Printing: 5 4 3 2 1   Year: 6 5 4 3 2

Printed in the United States of America

CONTENTS

Preface

Recently we have witnessed a tremendous proliferation of literature about the sexual abuse of children. Almost without exception, this literature focuses on two groups: male perpetrators of sex offenses against children and the youngsters who are victims of these sexual transgressions. We now know more about the nature and extent of both incestuous and nonincestuous offenses, the motivations and rationalizations of male offenders, and the impact of sex crimes on victims and families. We also are learning more about how to help victims and how to treat offenders. What has been referred to as "the best kept secret" is a secret no more: progress is being made.

Yet in reviewing this emerging body of literature, it is apparent that there is a serious omission. Almost nothing is written about women who commit incestuous and nonincestuous sex crimes. Moreover, little is known about the impact that female offenders have on their victims—particularly mothers who sexually abuse their offspring.

A true understanding of child sexual abuse demands that we seek answers to certain questions. What is the incidence of female sex offenses against children? What motivates women sex offenders? How do these women compare to male sex offenders? What are the consequences for male and female children if they are sexually victimized by their mothers or other adult females? How should these children and their female victimizers be treated in therapy? How do the courts respond to female sex offenders as compared with male offenders?

These and other important questions beg answers. Because the problem of female sex offenders has received little attention, knowledge in this area is anecdotal and often misleading. For example, there are no national studies of incidence. At best, therapists and others have been forced to rely on a few clinical studies. Court records are also limited and do not provide an adequate picture of the problem. Equally serious, cultural stereotypes underemphasize the possibility that women are motivated to commit sex crimes. Simply stated, very little is known about the problem.

But there is growing evidence that female-perpetrated sex offenses constitute a much bigger problem than we have been led to believe. In a sense, female sex offenders remain the "secret within the best kept secret." This book helps to reveal that secret by exposing the problem, by distinguishing fact from fiction, and by offering suggestions to therapists working with women offenders and their victims. The task is different than when working with male offenders and their victims. Both theory and the application of treatment models need to take those differences into account.

1
Explanations and Research

What do we know about female sex offenders? The answer is very little. There are few empirical studies of the extent of the problem. Moreover, arrest records seldom yield useful information because females rarely are charged with sex offenses other than prostitution. Even when charged with other sex crimes, women offenders nearly always plea bargain to lesser offenses.

Further compounding the problem are vague definitions of sexual abuse and a tendency to lump sex offenders together, thus overlooking important differences among them. Yet we do know this: power and control are common themes among male and female offenders alike. We know that age differences between victims and offenders are associated with abuses of power. We also know that both male and female offenders are likely to be much more knowledgeable and experienced in sexual behavior than their victims. Differences in age, knowledge and power make control through manipulation and coercion the common denominators for both male and female offenders.

Beyond this simple observation, not much information exists on female sex offenders. We must now begin to collect new data and to examine existing data about female molesters. We must first determine incidence, then seek to explain the dynamics of female-perpetrated sexual abuse, and finally attempt to develop effective treatment strategies for victims and offenders.

AN OVERVIEW OF RESEARCH

Adult and teenaged female molesters have not been studied extensively. A recent examination of the literature, for example, revealed almost no studies on female teenaged sex abusers. While the literature does contain scattered references to exhibitionism, sibling incest, kleptomania and prostitution[1] these deviations usually are presented in isolated, psychoanalytically-oriented case studies. As early as 1950, Pollack[2] was concerned that female sex offenses against children were a neglected area in criminological research.

Even in the literary world, female molesters have been under-represented. Webster and Masters (1963) present a cross section of fiction and drama dealing with incestuous relationships by well-known authors such as Mann, Maugham, Hawthorne, Gorky and Melville. Many of the selections deal with brother-sister incest. There is only one reference to a "pseudo-incestuous" situation involving a woman and her ex-husband's son in Pamela Frankeu's "Ask Me No More."

Davis and Leitenberg (1987)[3] could not locate a single study comparing male and female adolescent offenders. Wolfe[4] also reports that a review of the literature reveals almost no information on female sex offenders. In their 1977 literature review and annotated bibliography on sexual assault, Brodsky and Kelmack et al. cite only four references to female sex offenders.[5]

Until 1975, the Uniform Crime Report (UCR)[6] did not include data on female rapists. Since then, new legislation has provided for the incorporation of female and homosexual rape. In addition, the case of the Commonwealth of Massachusetts v. Denise Whitehead states that a female accessory to a male or female rape can be charged with rape.

The limited data available suggests that only a small percentage of sex offenders are female. Data from the Uniform Crime Report indicates that 8,683 adolescents under the age of eighteen were arrested in 1980-81 for forcible rape. Only two percent, or 149, of the teenagers arrested were female. All other sex offenses, excluding prostitution, involved a majority of male perpetrators (ninety-three percent).

During the late 1970's and early 1980's, a number of authorities anticipated that as figures for male sex offenders rose because of a growing awareness of the problem and because of increased reporting, the figures for female offenders would increase proportionately. Current statistical data indicate that these predictions were inaccurate.

Finkelhor[7] refers to the "male monopoly" on sexual abuse and notes that statistics support male predominance. Ninety percent of offenders are male and ninety-five percent of adult contacts with girls, and eight percent of those with boys, are by men.[8] According to Finkelhor,[9] women distinguish between sexual and nonsexual affection more accurately than men who are socially conditioned to sexualize children and who are more interested than women in the number of sex partners they have. Male self-esteem is related to sexual experiences. Women, on the other hand, are more empathic than men and are socially conditioned for the maternal role.

Groth[10] suggests that males use sex for retaliation and release of anger. Women, on the other hand, express anger by withholding sex. This, too, contributes to differences in male-female offender rates.

Thus, the consensus appears to be that male sex offenders far outnumber female. However, in view of the burgeoning number of sexual assaults perpetrated in all socioeconomic classes and by all age and ethnic groups, it seems likely that the true number of female offenders has not been disclosed. The number of female sex offenders probably is much higher than is suggested by arrest estimates.

A 1980 survey of 1735 female and male parochial and public school tenth graders in several midwestern communities revealed that there is a subculture of deviance involving both sexes.[11] This study suggested that teenage girls engage less frequently than males in delinquency, but they did not specialize in "female crimes." Moreover, similar factors influenced the behaviors of both males and females. The study also revealed that 4.8% of the boys admitted to sexually assaultive behavior as compared to 3.3% of the females. Surprisingly, 4.7% of the males were involved in prostitution as compared to .2% of the females. Pollack's studies also indicate no specificity of female crimes.[12]

Two other recent studies highlight the significance of female molesters. David Finkelhor of the University of New Hampshire conducted a nationwide survey (1983-85) involving 270 cases of sexual abuse. Among other conclusions, Finkelhor found that women committed forty percent of all child sexual abuse in daycare settings, thus dispelling the myth that female pedophiles are rare.[13]

The second study involved eighty-three incarcerated rapists. Petrovich and Templar found that fifty-nine percent of these men had been heterosexually molested in their youth and that eight-two percent of the cases involved intercourse. In twenty-one percent of the cases, the female molesters were in the role of nurturer or protector.[14] What is clear from this study is that there appears to be a higher rate of sexual assault by women than has heretofore been suspected.

Under-Representing and Under-Reporting

There are many reasons why adolescent and adult female perpetrators appear to be under-represented in the overall population of sex offenders. There also are important reasons why those females who do molest children remain undetected.

Contemporary norms and values in the United States and Canada exacerbate sexual acting-out in many males. As a group, males are socialized to openly express aggression from infancy, and to sexualize their feelings of rage and impotence. In addition, it is argued that our society is patriarchal in the sense that many males continue to practice a double standard sexually, to claim ownership of less powerful females, and to exercise a cultural prerogative to displace aggression onto powerless persons such as women and children.

In contrast, most females do not sexualize relationships, eroticize anger or associate power and control with sexual needs. Thus, sexually aggressive acts are not a common vehicle for expression of displaced anger among women.

Females who do sexually abuse children remain largely undetected. Special population groups of offenders are harder for society to acknowledge due to dissonant cultural views. Women, children and developmentally disabled persons are perceived by society as vulnerable and, therefore, incapable of the aggression associated with able-bodied males. These groups of offenders are under-reported, minimized, or denied.

Groth[15] believes that women mask sex offenses and also may be involved more in incest which is less frequently reported than out-of-home molestation. Groth also believes that when women do molest males, the males are less likely to disclose abuse.

Western culture supports a wide range of physical behaviors among females, such as hugging, touching, hand-holding and affectionate kissing, that may or may not include sexual elements or have sexual overtones.[16] For males, the culture supports a much narrower repertoire of behaviors that express affection physically. Thus, for males, there is a clearer demarcation between abusive and nonabusive behaviors; there is less likelihood of their rationalizing inappropriate behavior.[17]

Another factor limiting the disclosure of female perpetration relates to society's persistent denial of abusive behaviors. In general, victimization is minimized, and particularly abhorrent types of abuse, such as those involving a mother and child, or a teenaged girl and toddler, tend to be denied.

Society does not perceive females as abusers; they are stereotyped as physically and psychologically incapable of victimizing. Feminists, especially, may be reluctant to acknowledge the existence of abusive behaviors among females. They fear that those cases that do exist will be publicized disproportionately in order to minimize and justify male offenses.

Prosecution

Because cases involving female offenders are difficult to prosecute criminally, they often do not reach the attention of the public. The following example is an illustration. A twenty-eight-year-old male teacher in Maricopa County, Arizona, recently was sentenced to twelve years in prison for abducting and sexually molesting a fourteen-year-old female student who stated that the relationship was consensual. During that same period of time, another case in Arizona was dismissed against a thirty-year-old female teacher who had been charged with sexually abusing a thirteen-year-old male student.

Reckless and Kay[18] attribute the minimization of female offenses to the "Chivalry Hypothesis" (i.e., the notion that female victims and the courts are lenient toward women by virtue of the fact that they are females). Feyerherm and Pope (1980) found that the juvenile courts are lenient with females for nonstatus offenses but harsh for status offenses.[19]

To further confuse the issue, it often is not feasible to prosecute female perpetrators. Jurors tend to minimize female offenses, perhaps because of their own sense of abhorrence and denial, thus lessening the likelihood of conviction. In incest cases, abuse can involve collusion—and sometimes active participation—between parents. This makes it even more difficult to prosecute and convict the primary offender. Charges usually are reduced considerably through the plea bargaining process. Often, female partners in intrafamilial molestation cases are charged with very minor offenses that are plea bargained to misdemeanors. In such cases it would be "fiscally irresponsible" to attempt prosecution.

In addition, siblings of victims and extended family members need mothers at home, especially when fathers are incarcerated. In one case, for example, an adult male offender sodomized and vaginally penetrated his fourteen-year-old daughter for two years. The mother participated in the abuse. Multiple offenses were committed as the perpetrator shared a bed with both his wife and daughter. On several occasions, he verbally coerced and manipulated his wife to participate in acts of vaginal fondling, breast fondling, and digital penetration of their daughter. The offender, a wealthy building contractor charged with several Class 2 felonies, hired an excellent defense attorney who secured a plea to one count of a Class 6 felony, a charge equivalent to a misdemeanor. When the prosecutor was asked why he did not charge the mother, he replied, "With what? She did less than he did. What could I charge her with—a minor misdemeanor? It's not worth it. And she has two other kids at home who need her."

Another reason why female sex offenses remain hidden relates to shame and embarrassment. There appears to be a stigma resulting from molestation by a female perpetrator that precludes disclosure even to persons the victim trusts.

CLINICAL AND NONCLINICAL EXPLANATIONS

There have been several anecdotal and qualitative clinical studies on female molesters in the last few years. The data should be reviewed with caution.

Self-reports based on a relatively small number of clinical interviews are a large part of the data available to clinicians. Self-reports are not always a valid indicator of behavior; they are particularly unreliable when the focus is on criminal or socially unacceptable behavior. In addition, the accuracy of self-reports generally is contingent on the expertise and experience of the interviewers. An extensive background in the complex dynamics of abuse is an invaluable prerequisite for interviewers. Both male and female sex offenders rationalize, minimize and deny their behaviors. They are reluctant to self-disclose because the result, at best, is social censure and, at worst, criminal prosecution.

On the other hand, there is a growing but limited body of clinically-obtained information and systematically-gathered research evidence emerging in the literature. Groth (1981) and Finkelhor (1986) both elaborate on issues related to female molestation. Groth suggests that women sex offenders exist in greater numbers than has been suspected. The reasons are as follows:

- women mask deviance under the guise of socially acceptable behaviors

- women who commit incestuous offenses are reported less frequently than those who commit extrafamilial sex crimes

- women tend to sexually abuse boys who are reluctant to disclose.

Groth[20] believes that both female and male molestation involve similar dynamics in which nonsexual needs are met through molestation. Nevertheless, the etiology underlying male and female offenders differs in that women generally do not use sex to retaliate and to release anger.

Finkelhor[21] also discusses the male monopoly on sexual abuse despite the fact that some authorities[22] challenge this assumption by citing the cultural bias against perceiving women as child molesters. Like Groth, Finkelhor supports the notion that women generally abuse at the instigation of men. Moreover, ninety-five percent of adult sexual abuse with girls, and eighty percent of adult sexual abuse with boys, is perpetrated by men.[23]

Finkelhor elaborates on the reasons for the predominance of male offenders. In general, he believes that men are used to a position of dominance, especially with young persons, and that they seek sexual variety divorced from emotions. Male self-esteem is linked to sexual prowess and many men do not distinguish between sexual and non-sexual needs. Women, on the other hand, are conditioned to empathize and to assume the maternal role.

Carmen, Reiker and Mills[24] report that men act out victimization while women turn their feelings inward. Hence, many adult males, molested as children, act out aggressively through criminal offenses, including sex crimes. They comprise a large portion of the criminal population. Females, on the other hand, internalize anger and pain through chronic depression or suicide attempts. As a result, fifty-three percent of female psychiatric inpatients were molested as children (compared with twenty-three percent of male inpatients).

Haugaard and Reppucci[25] agree with other authorities regarding the predominance of male offenders, noting that reports of both mother-daughter and mother-son incest are rare, with few clinical or large-scale surveys. Existing reports describe mother-son incest with absent fathers and lonely, seductive mothers seeking substitutes for their spouses.

Groth, Finkelhor, Forward and the other authorities cited above base their observations on vast clinical experience and expertise with abusing populations. As experts, their opinions merit credibility. In recent years, however, other authorities have begun to examine specific samples of abusing women in an attempt to formulate data-based hypotheses regarding prevalence, etiology and dynamics. For the most part, these studies have been short-term with small sample sizes and inconclusive findings.

Knopp and Lackey surveyed forty-four treatment providers for female sex offenders to compile data on evaluation methods, psychological assessment and research issues as well as specific information regarding client populations (numbers of co-perpetrators, types of offenses, etc.). The focus of the survey was noncritical although the information gathered is useful in demonstrating treatment approaches currently in use in the United States.

Mathews et al. conducted an exploratory, qualitative study based on a sample of sixteen women drawn from a community correctional facility in Minneapolis, Minnesota.[26] They describe three types of female offenders: 1) the teacher-lover who becomes involved with pre-adolescent and adolescent males; 2) the predisposed or intergenerational offender, a victim herself, who initiates molestation of her own children; and 3) the dependent male-coerced offender who sexually abuses in and out of the home. In general, all of the sixteen women disclosed early histories of sexual abuse and the majority were disciplined harshly as children.

Wolfe[27] reports on twelve adult female molesters who were psychologically evaluated and clinically interviewed. In contrast to male molesters, genital orgasm was not a motivator for the deviant behavior of these women. They made few attempts to entice child victims to manipulate adult genitals. These women began molesting at a later age than their male counterparts. In fifty percent of the cases, adult male partners helped engage in the assaults. Dependence (on males) was used as a defense mechanism along with projection, denial and rationalization. Like male molesters, the women were socially isolated, did not generally use physical force with their victims, and fantasized about the offense.

Other data from the study revealed that fifty-eight percent of the women had been sexually abused as children. Many of them were chemical abusers and sexually dysfunctional. Only one of the women was clinically diagnosed as psychotic. Fifty percent of the offenses involved homosexual pedophilia and the majority of the offenses were intrafamilial. In general, the offenders lacked empathy for their victims.

Wolfe's study, albeit small, yields some interesting information. Some popular notions are not supported in the sample (i.e., that women have victim empathy or that many female molesters are psychotic). However, the sample is small and much of the data is based on self-reports. For example, the women reported that their first offenses occurred during adulthood. It is likely offenses began earlier.

A comparison of Wolfe's study with one of comparable size in Phoenix, Arizona, during 1985-88,[28] reveals both similar and contrasting information. In the Phoenix sample, five of the eleven adult female molesters had been evaluated and clinically diagnosed as Borderline Personality Disorder or psychotic. Three of the eleven offenders had partners or co-assailants who allegedly forced the women to sexually abuse their daughters. As in Wolfe's study, the women engaged in genital manipulation and insertion of objects into their victims. Homosexual molestation was common among all eleven perpetrators.

None of the perpetrators initiated disclosures and the women used the characteristic defenses of denial, projection, minimization and rationalization. Since denial was a common defense, it was difficult to ascertain when offending behaviors began for these women. All offenses were intrafamilial and in only seven was alcohol a contributing factor. As in Wolfe's sample, empathic responses were absent. It would be unlikely to expect victim empathy in this character-disordered/borderline population. In general, the women functioned marginally in all areas, including interpersonally and sexually.

SUMMARY AND CRITIQUE

Little information is known about female sexual assault. Until recently, the literature generally did not recognize women as perpetrators.

Methodology

The few current studies that do exist are short-term with small sample sizes. Information was gathered through self-reports which often are neither reliable nor valid. Findings are tentative, hypothetical and contradictory, yielding more questions than answers:

1.   If, as Groth and Finkelhor suggest, women sexually abuse at the instigation of men, what is the underlying dynamic? Is polymorphous perversity (i.e., voyeurism and exhibitionism) involved? Are the deviant acts just another objectification and victimization of women by men with children serving as vehicles for this victimization?

2.   Does Finkelhor's study of daycare settings indicate that women generally molest very young children more often than older ones?

3.   If, as Pollack suggests, there is no specificity of female crimes, how large a number of "hidden" female sex offenses are there?   Has cultural denial hidden vast numbers of these offenders?   Will this denial create biases in therapeutic approaches so that serious offenses by women will be minimized during the treatment process?

4.   If, as Groth suggests, some males use sex as a vehicle for release of anger, while women express anger by withholding sex, what are the underlying motives for female sex offenses? Are the needs always nonsexual?

5.   Petrovitch and Templar's study of male rapists heterosexually abused in childhood suggests that molestation by females sometimes results in rage in male victims. Female victims of molestation react differently. Is this difference just another reflection of the inordinate anger harbored by many males? Is it a reflection of men's need to eroticize anger or the need for men to seek release through acting-out behavior?

6.   Is there an accurate typology for female sex offenders?

7.   Is the fact that women often are coerced by men to commit sex offenses a reflection of dependence or victimization?

8.   At what age do most women perpetrators begin the commission of sex offenses?

Theory

Thus far, there is no well-established theory or data regarding female sex offenders and their offenses. Hence, generalizations must be viewed with skepticism. However, current data consistently indicates that:

1.   women sex offenders are increasing in the clinical population;

2.   homosexual molestation appears to be more common among female molesters than among male molesters;

3.   assaults involving partners are typical of female molestation and often involve coercion by male accomplices; and,

4.   there are similarities and differences between female and male perpetration (i.e., defenses used, power dynamics, objectification of victims, histories involving sexual victimization in childhood, etc.).

These findings are important in establishing a base for beginning to understand the etiology and dynamics of female molestation. The findings also demonstrate the pressing need for understanding prevalence and differing classification of female molestation.

Notes: Chapter One

1. Refer to Schlesinger, L.J. and Revitch, E. (Eds.), 1983 for elaboration.

2. Pollack, O., (1950), 1961, 26.

3. Davis, G.E. and Leitenberg, H., 1987, 421.

4. Wolfe, F. A., March 1985, 1.

5. Among the few references to mother-child incest in the literature are: Wahl, C.W., 1960, 188; Walters, D.R., 1975, 122; Justice, B. and Justice, R., 1979, 193; and Groth, A.N., March 15, 1982, 230. Warren, M.Q., 1981, 9, notes that there is a need for data regarding the characteristics of all female offenders.

6. The UCR or Uniform Crime Report is published annually by the U.S. Department of Justice and includes arrest records reported throughout the country by police jurisdictions.

7. Finkelhor, D., 1986, 126.

8. Finkelhor, D. and Russell, D., 1984, 171-87.

9. Finkelhor, D., 1981, 185-6.

10. Groth, A.N., 1981, 185-6.

11. Figueira-McDonough, J., Barton, W.H., and Sarri, R.C., 1981, 20-44.

12. Pollack, O., 1950, 1961, 2.

13. Reported in the Arizona Republic, March 22, 1988, from U.P. International, "Home's Abuse Risk Tops Daycare's, Study Says;" also refer to Finkelhorn D., and Williams, L.M., 1988.

14. Petrovitch, M. and Templar, D.I., 1984, 810.

15. Groth, A.N., 1981, 191.

16. Breast feeding is encouraged in the United States for health and the emotional well-being of both mother and child. Yet, nursing is a sensual experience that can, for some mothers, result in orgasm. Mothers in the United States have been known to nurse their toddlers to age three or four. It is interesting that prolonged nursing has not been perceived as a deviant sexual practice.

17. Male sex offenders do, indeed, deny, minimize and rationalize abuse. However, physical touching tends to be proscribed for males (outside of the sexual context with consenting adults). Hence, there is less likelihood for rationalization among males than among females in general.

18. Reckless, W. and Kay, B., 1967,16.

19. Feyerherm, W.H. and Pope, C., 1980.

20. A status offense involves activities designated as criminal only by virtue of the age of the offender. Runaway behavior and school truancy are status offenses.

21. Groth, A.N., 1981.

22. Finkelhor, D., 1986, 126.

23. Sgroi, S., is one of the authorities who challenges this assumption, 1982, 39-79.

24. Finkelhor, D., and Russell, D., 1984.

25. Carmen, E., Reiker, P.P., and Mills, T., 1984, 378-83.

26. Haugaard, J.J. and Reppucci, N.D., 1988, 128.

27. Knopp, F.H., and Lackey, L.B., 1987.

28. Mathews, R., Mathews, J.K., and Speltz, K., 1980. The authors of
     this study concluded that only one of the sixteen women sampled
     was severely psychologically disturbed (depressed, suicidal,
     antisocial or paranoid). However, the study describes the
     predisposed/intergenerational abusers as having elevated scores on
     scales 4, 6, 7, 8, and 9 of the Minnesota Multiphasic Personality
     Inventory. They are often chemically abusive.

2
TYPES OF WOMEN
OFFENDERS

There are different categories of male and female offenders which overlap (e.g., incestuous, pedophilic, sadistic). Some authorities believe the typology involves a continuum rather than separate categories. While distinctions sometimes appear to be arbitrary, they also are useful in providing an understanding of the various offenses.

FEMALE RAPISTS

There is very little data on female rapists, partly because the majority of female sex offenses are intrafamilial and nonviolent (Groth, 1981).[1] Groth acknowledges the existence of female rape but believes that statistically this crime is negligible, partly because women do not manifest rage and frustration in sex offenses.[2] Marvasti concurs that sexual assault by women usually is nonviolent.[3] However, as with other sex offenses, female rape probably is under-reported and minimized for the same reasons that female molestation in general is denied in the United States.

Brown, Hull and Panesis studied twenty females charged with rape.[4] While their conclusions are tentative (based on incomplete data and a small sample size) results point to some similarities between female and male rapists. For example, like male rapists, the majority of the women sampled were between the ages of seventeen and twenty-four, knew their victims and perpetrated the assaults in the home. Thirty percent of the women (compared to thirty-three percent of the males) were convicted of the crime in criminal courts.

Of particular interest and relevance to future studies were findings showing that in 27.3% of the cases, a weapon was used;[5] in 76,5% of the cases, victims were female (homosexual rape); and in 57.1% of the cases, victims were juveniles as young as three years of age (i.e., much younger than offenders).

FEMALE SEXUAL HARASSMENT

Female sexual harassers are placed on a continuum. Verbal and physical harassers are on one end; rapists and sexual assaulters are on the other end. In their study of sexual harassment in the workplace, Backhouse and Cohen interviewed males to determine the existence or degree of harassment by women.[6] The authors report that the majority of men interviewed were eager to discuss harassment which typically was perceived as flattering or humorous. Many of the men fantasized about women harassing them. Women did not use coercion nor were their job positions secure enough for them to threaten male employees with reprisals such as demotions, dismissals or loss of job-related benefits. Some of the men, however, experienced many of the same symptoms as female victims such as embarrassment, tension, frustration, apprehension and generalized emotional discomfort.[7]

Backhouse and Cohen attribute differences in sexual harassment by men and by women to traditional sex roles where females are passive and powerless, both psychologically and economically. They also note that since men have been securing employment in traditional female jobs such as flight attendants, nurses and secretaries, they are starting to experience the same harassment as women. In the final analysis, female harassment is perceived as negligible because of a cultural denial that women can exert sexual power over males.

Case Example

The following case example illustrates the complicated dynamics in female assaultive behavior. It involves a forty-year-old man charged with sexually abusing two girls, his fifteen-year-old stepdaughter and her thirteen-year-old friend. Joe steadfastly maintained that the girls had molested him. He claimed that one girl grabbed his penis and began to masturbate him while the other kissed him "all over, leaving hickies" and forced him to engage in cunnilingus and fellatio. Joe admitted that the abuse both aroused and frightened him.

Joe presented himself as an angry, life-long victim of females. Women frightened him by their aggressive behavior. He reported that teenaged girls whistled, grabbed his "butt" and propositioned him. When he walked through his office, secretaries riveted their eyes on his groin.

Joe was raised by his mother and older sister since birth. His mother worked to support the children, entrusting Joe's care to his twelve-year-old sister who dressed him in female clothing until he was five, and later sexually abused him (fondled his genitals) until he was thirteen.

Like many male child victims, Joe experienced ambivalent feelings about the abuse. He felt guilty about the pleasurable aspects of incest with his sister. Still, he was angry at, and confused by, the victimization. When his sister left home during Joe's thirteenth year, he felt resentful and abandoned. At sixteen, he joined the Navy. Joe married five times, but was never able to form close interpersonal relationships with women; he experienced intermittent periods of impotence. Two of Joe's wives claimed that he beat them. Joe stated that he acted in self-defense, alleging that his wives were violent and dangerous. He claimed he had to strike them following their unprovoked episodes of verbal and physical assaults against him.

Joe presents an interesting case study of the complicated dynamics involved in abusive relationships. He was seductive and charming with females who found his demeanor, therefore, disarming and challenging in that he was not an aggressive male. Often, teenaged girls and women did, in fact, harass Joe, sometimes mockingly and sadistically and, sometimes, assertively or aggressively with an intent to seduce.

Over the years, Joe began to react to the attentiveness of women by using the defense of fantasized projection. He totally identified with a victim position because of the role he played as a child. Yet he harbored rage against females and an unconscious desire to be the powerful aggressor. By the time Joe reached middle age, he began to openly manifest aggression toward females. Unable to accept this aspect of himself, he projected his feelings outwardly onto females, accusing them of thoughts he harbored and behaviors he manifested.

In therapy, Joe was confronted with the reality of his passive acceptance of seduction by two teenaged girls, girls he easily could have resisted had he not wished to abuse them. In the end, this difficult client could not relinquish the victim role with which he totally identified and without which he might have experienced psychological decompensation.

MOTHER MOLESTERS

There are several types of mother molesters. Abuse scenarios vary, depending on such factors as age and sex preferences. Some women molest only their son(s), while a surprisingly large number of mothers molest daughters or children of both sexes. In some instances, mothers derive vicarious or voyeuristic pleasure by coercing their children to engage in sibling incest.

Both parents may be involved in the molestation of their children. Couples have been arrested for involving their children in pornography and prostitution. In one case, a woman had intercourse with her teenaged daughter's boyfriend. Thereafter, the girl was forced to engage in sexual relations with her boyfriend while the mother watched.

McCarty examined the characteristics of twenty-six mothers who molested their own children.[8] Her typology included the independent offender, the co-offender and the accomplice. In general, the offenders were raised in dysfunctional homes where sexual and physical abuse was prevalent. The women married young and were employed, although only the women with co-offenders worked at home. As expected, the independent offenders were characterized as autonomous (i.e., not dependent on males). Sixty percent of the independent offenders sexually abused their daughters, while the others abused both sons and daughters.[9] The women with co-offenders, unlike the other two types, tended to be borderline intellectually and were married several times—factors which lend credence to the notion that they were dependent women under the influence of men.

The independent female offenders in this study appeared to be more emotionally disturbed than the other two types. They were in crisis at the time of the molestation, abused drugs and violated very young victims. Seventy-eight percept of the independent offenders were sexually abused by brothers, while women with co-offenders were abused by primary caretakers.[10] McCarty believes that none of the offenders was fixated.

Mother-Son Incest

The clinical literature on mother-child incest is rare before the 1970's. For example, experts such as Herman[11] cite the rarity of mother-son molestation, noting that there are only thirty documented cases in the literature, eight of which involve the son raping the mother.[12] Haugaard and Reppucci concur with Herman, noting that there is a greater taboo against mother-son incest than against father-daughter abuse, and that there have been few clinical reports or instances of this type of molestation in any of the large-scale surveys.[13] However, in the scattered references to mother-son incest in the literature, mothers are treated lightly since only male abusers are seen as capable of aggression.

Forward notes that this form of abuse can be subtly traumatic and involves complicated dynamics. In ninety-five percent of the cases, the father is absent and the mother maneuvers her son into a quasi-spousal role, seeking both sexual and emotional satisfaction from the child. The son experiences a wide array of emotions including guilt, desire, love and hate. Guilt stemming from participation and physical enjoyment interferes with the boy's capacity for establishing normal relationships in the future. According to Forward, sons molested by their mothers may become impotent, homosexual, rapists, daughter or wife abusers, or even murderers.[14]

Forward also identifies three patterns or levels of mother-son molestation. In the first, there is no overt sexual contact but, rather, physical and emotional intimacy. The son becomes overly attached to his mother, experiencing erotic dreams and isolating himself from others. He moves into the father's role but with sexual frustration. This form of abuse can lead to impotence and fear of women.

Nonintercourse, which involves seduction leading to acts such as mutual masturbation, is the second level of abuse and may be as traumatic as actual intercourse (the third level). Haugaard and Reppucci report that the few existing studies on mother-son incest describe the mothers as promiscuous and alcoholic. The sons are past puberty at the time of the abuse and are symbiotically linked to their mothers.[15] In other words, there is a mutual interdependence between the mothers and sons. The father is absent and the son has witnessed sexual acts between his mother and her lovers. Justice concurs, noting that the adolescent male assumes the role of the absent father and provides substitute gratification for the mother.[16]

Groth describes a case involving a mother who molested her two sons starting when they each were ten years of age. She was not psychotic and her I.Q. was not limited. Abused as a child, this woman experienced conflicts surrounding dependency, autonomy, vulnerability and rage. Sex became an arena for acting out these conflicts. Sex alleviated this woman's depression and gave her a sense of self-worth. It offered her a chance to recapitulate her own molestation. It also afforded her an opportunity to degrade her spouse since her boys may have symbolized their father.[17]

Mother-Daughter Incest

Authorities also concur that mother-daughter incest is rare; only a few instances are cited in the literature.[18] In her sample of 930, Russell found only one victim of mother-daughter molestation.[19]

Forward notes that mother-daughter molestation is the least understood form of abuse. She describes the women as very disturbed and possibly psychotic, who perceive their daughters as extensions of themselves. These women are infantile with poor ego boundaries. They reverse roles with their daughters, turning to children—sometimes as early as during infancy—for emotional nurturance and support. Sex becomes a masturbatory act for self-stimulation. The daughter's function is to "mother" the parent. The backgrounds of these women often are fraught with abuse and neglect.[20]

TRIADS

One distinguishing feature of female molestation is the high percentage of cases where male partners or accomplices are involved. The triad in mother-child incest involves a victim, male partner and female abuser.[21] The triad in father-child incest includes a victim, collusive mother and male abuser. Possibly because of the common features shared by most incestuous families (i.e., multiple dysfunctions and pervasive problems), there are many similarities between the triads involving fathers and mothers who sexually abuse their children.

Figure 1
TRIADS

**Father (Partner/
step-father) Perpetrator**

Mother colludes (silent
partner); actively abandons
child; seeks nurturing;
is regressed/dependent;
rationalizes; minimizes;
denies; projects;
vicariously re-enacts
own abuse; (abuses
chemicals)

Father victimizes; seeks
nurturing; is regressed/
dependent; rationalizes;
minimizes; denies; manipulates; objectifies others;
has low frustration tolerance; (abuses chemicals)

Victim plays martyr role;
protects parents; acts as
pseudo-adult

Mother Perpetrator

Mother victimizes (with
co-partner); suffers learned
helplessness and/or hostility
toward child; seeks nurturing;
is regressed/dependent;
rationalizes; minimizes;
projects; vicariously re-enacts
own abuse (or identifies with
aggressor); (abuses chemicals)

Father coerces and/or
colludes (secondary victimization); seeks nurturing
is regressed/dependent;
rationalizes; minimizes; denies;
manipulates; objectifies others;
has low frustration tolerance;
(abuses chemicals)

Victim plays martyr role;
protects parents; acts as
pseudo-adult

Family enmeshed; multi-faceted
dysfunctions; socially
isolated; secretive;
collusive; inter-dependent

Mothers

In both father-child and mother-child incest, many of the mothers are dependent, regressed personalities who tend to use the defense mechanisms of rationalization, minimization, denial and projection. Silent or collusive mothers expend considerable energy minimizing or denying their spouses' offenses. They do so in order to preserve the status quo on which they depend both for their livelihood and for their emotional stability.

Mothers who molest often are dependent on partner-abusers. These mothers also minimize, deny and rationalize abusive behaviors to preserve the status quo and their fragile self-esteem, and to avoid interference from the police or child protective service agencies. Both types of mothers (i.e., those who abuse and those who collude) sometimes are chemically-addicted, or are involved with partners who are alcoholic or drug addicts.

Both abusing and colluding mothers seek nurturing and mothering through a reversal of roles in the family. The incestuous mother seeks to meet (nonsexual) needs for affection and emotional warmth by molesting her child. The silent partner mother (inadvertently) places her daughter in the role of wife and parent. Both types of mothers often were victimized as children. In many cases, they vicariously re-enact their own trauma in the hope of mastery. In some cases, the collusive mother may identify with her victim-daughter while the incestuous mother may identify with her original aggressor.

Behaviorally, the two types of mothers respond differently to their dysfunctional backgrounds. The incestuous mother tends to become a victimizer; the silent partner, a colluder. Silent partners condone incest; incestuous mothers become molesters or partners in molestation. Finally, both the incestuous mother who molests with her spouse, and the collusive mother, sometimes operate from positions of learned helplessness. Like battered women, they allow themselves to be dominated and controlled by their partners. Both types of mothers, however, actively abandon their daughters. They choose between security and autonomy (i.e., they support their spouses or partners at

the expense of their children). One type of mother allows abuse; the
other participates in it.

Fathers and Partners

Men often encourage or coerce their spouses to molest. These
fathers often abuse alcohol or drugs. Many of these men suffer from
sexual dysfunctions and have problems with anger management. Like
the women, they use the defenses of denial, minimization,
rationalization and projection. Incestuous and co-partner fathers deny
their offenses or project responsibility onto their wives. Collusive
fathers also project responsibility and deny their role in
mother-daughter molestation.

Victims

The child victim becomes the family martyr or sacrificial lamb,
regardless of which parent is the molester. The child is responsible for
maintenance of the status quo in the home. When Mom molests and
Dad is the co-partner, or collusive enabler, the daughter or son's role is
to nurture and protect the mother, both from disclosure and from Dad.
When Dad is the abuser, the child protects him from detection and
protects Mom from explicit knowledge of abuse. Often, the female child
victim becomes the nurturing wife for Dad and the responsible
mother-homemaker for Mom.

CASE EXAMPLES

1.   Janet was diagnosed psychotic and hospitalized periodically
        during her thirty-three years. She was a victim of sexual
        and physical abuse by multiple perpetrators since infancy.
        She molested her sons who were placed in long-term foster
        care by child protective services following disclosure during
        one of Janet's numerous hospitalizations.

Janet received SSI disability payments because she was not employable due to her emotional problems. She had a wide array of therapists to provide her with supportive interventions. Psychotropic medication and various other drugs were prescribed for her physical problems which included asthma, eczema and ulcerative colitis. Although a bisexual, Janet rarely was sexually involved with adult male partners. Her sons were surrogate lovers whom she used to meet her sexual and emotional needs.

2. Denise, twenty-nine with an I.Q. of sixty-nine, did not remember her childhood. A depressed woman who gave birth to her first child out of wedlock at age fifteen, Denise received AFDC (Aid to Families with Dependent Children) to support her family. She did not work and had a number of boyfriends.

Denise's oldest child, Carol, resembled her mother physically and the two were close—a closeness enhanced by Denise's narcissistic identification with her child. When Carol was thirteen, her mother's live-in boyfriend began to molest her. He also asked Denise if she would agree to three-way sex with Carol and himself. One night, Denise, Carol and Jerry drank beer together and engaged in group sex. Denise performed cunnilingus on her daughter who reported the offense to a neighbor. Denise admitted the molestation to the police, although she alleged that Jerry forced her at gunpoint to abuse her daughter. She subsequently was charged with two counts of child sexual abuse, later reduced to one count of attempted sexual abuse. Denise served three months in county jail. The plea bargain also involved five years probation, mandated therapy, a "no-contact order" with children under the age of eighteen, and mandated attendance of an alcohol rehabilitation program.

Carol was placed in long-term foster care. She remained
loyal to her mother and angry that the "system" would not
allow her to visit or live with Denise. She refused to deal
with the molestation in therapy, insisting Denise was
coerced into sexual contact with her. Carol acted out
sexually in her foster home, both with male and female
foster siblings. At age fourteen, she was suspended from
school following an episode where she was found in the
locker room engaging in oral sex with a twelve-year-old
male. Carol was evaluated psychologically and diagnosed a
developing Borderline Personality Disorder.

3.   Bill, thirty-seven, and his wife, Sarah, thirty, were in
couples therapy following disclosure of sexual abuse of their
eleven year old twin girls. Bill had sexually abused the girls
from their third to eleventh years, forcing fellatio,
cunnilingus and group sex. The girls reported the abuse to
Sarah on numerous occasions, but she accused them of
fabrication and took no action. Finally, one twin disclosed
to the mother of her friend who alerted the police.

There had been several prior referrals to child protective
services for physical abuse of one of the twins and of the
couple's eight year old son, Mark. Her social worker
described Sarah as a perfectionist, short-tempered and
mentally dull. Psychological evaluations of both parents
revealed antisocial features, sexual dysfunctions, passivity
and high stressors (employment instability, multiple moves,
etc.). Bill was diagnosed as Antisocial Personality Disorder;
Sarah, as Borderline Personality Disorder. Bill's I.Q. was
ninety-two; Sarah's, seventy-four.

Following disclosure, the girls were placed in foster care
since Sarah did not believe their allegations and since Bill
remained in the home pending the outcome of the criminal
proceedings. The couple was referred to a group for sex
offenders and their wives; the twins were seen by another
therapist to work through issues related to trauma,
rejection and abandonment; and Mark was seen by still a
third therapist for support.

Sarah initially did well in therapy as she began to understand how her own abusive background affected her, particularly with reference to parenting. Her mother had abandoned her soon after birth. She subsequently was molested by her father until placed in foster care at age five. Thereafter, Sarah lived in a series of foster and group homes. In three of the homes, she was both physically and sexually abused. Her traumatic background involving abuse and abandonment resulted in Sarah's severe personality deficits. She was unable to bond with or nurture her children (i.e., provide the parenting that she, herself, never received). Controlled hostility, unmet dependency needs and unresolved trauma were major therapeutic issues requiring resolution.

After several months of therapy, Sarah asked Bill to leave the home in preparation for the girls to return. A few days after Bill left, Sarah became enraged by Mark who pouted constantly over the loss of his father. Sarah used the family's "board of education" as a disciplinary measure. When Mark struggled to free himself from his mother, he was struck on the arm. His therapist subsequently noticed the bruise on Mark's arm and reported the incident. Mark was placed in a foster home where, almost immediately, he tried to fondle the genitals of his three-year-old foster sibling. His behavior was attributed to stress and over-exposure to sexual stimuli (Bill's X-rated movies), and was controlled by environmental manipulation.

Several weeks later, during a group therapy session in which the children were asked what changes they wanted from their parents, Mark announced, "I want my Mom to stop touching and frenching me." Subsequent disclosures revealed that Sarah had been molesting her son for three years.

Clinical Impressions

Sarah, an antisocial personality, attempted to manipulate her son and the system for her own benefit. The other two women were highly dysfunctional with guarded to poor prognoses. Personality disorganization and low mental functioning precluded the likelihood of insight incorporation antecedent to behavioral change.

In some ways, the three female molesters resemble many male offenders. These women lacked empathic responses and did not appear to experience guilt or remorse for their actions. They had low impulse control and low frustration tolerance. Like many male offenders, these women were abused as children, objectified other people and sexualized their relationships. However, many male offenders appear to present more solid personality integration than these women. For this reason, they often are perceived as treatable in the sense that their compulsions or addictions can be controlled rather than cured. These women, on the other hand, seemed likely to respond only to external controls, medication, superficial support and environmental manipulation without the possibility of lasting behavioral changes

HOMOSEXUAL MOLESTATION

The etiology and dynamics of homosexual molestation remain unknown. Further methodologically-sound research with adequate sample sizes is needed before theories can be formulated. Existing data, however, indicates that homosexual abuse by female perpetrators is not uncommon.

Among the twenty-six cases studied by McCarty, sixty percent of the independent (without partner participation) female sex offenders molested their daughters.[22] In Brown, Hull and Panesis's study of twenty females charged with rape, the majority of the offenses involved homosexual assault.[23] Wolfe, found that homosexual assault was common in his sample of twelve adult female intrafamilial molesters.[24]

On the basis of existing clinical studies and information regarding sexual deviance in general, certain hypotheses regarding etiology and types of homosexual offenders can be proposed. These hypotheses are presented in order to help therapists begin to understand the multifaceted, complicated dynamics involved when assessing female molestation; to distinguish among treatable and nontreatable offenders; and to formulate tentative management or treatment strategies.

Latent Homosexuality

Unconscious or suppressed homosexual tendencies can be expressed and rationalized in same sex child molestation under the umbrella of sexual abuse in general or when coercion by a male partner is involved. In other words, a woman can molest a female child under the guise of random selection (indiscriminate choice) or by asserting that she was forced into homosexual selection by her male partner. For some adults, molestation is more ego syntonic than homosexuality.

One striking characteristic of a number of female and male child molesters is a distorted value system, based on a rigid defensive structure that tolerates certain aberrant behaviors, but not others. Therapists who have treated male sex offenders, for example, note the astonishment of their clients at the suggestion that an extramarital affair might be preferable to incestuous abuse of a child. These men insist that their wives, who remain faithful to them following the disclosure of incest, would have killed them had they engaged in adultery. Some cite passages from the Bible prohibiting adulterous relations. They also condemn homosexuality as both immoral and unnatural.

Perhaps society has more openly condemned homosexuality and adultery than child molestation. Regardless, it is reasonable to assume that some female child molesters are, in fact, latent homosexuals either unable or unwilling to accept their sexual identities.

Marvasti provides an example of a possible latent homosexual who finds release in child molestation. The author describes a female molester in her mid-forties with homosexual tendencies. A victim of molestation by her own mother, this woman's adult sexual partner accused her of acting seductively toward her own daughter and of sexualizing the mother-child relationship.[25]

Shelly, a client in therapy in her late thirties with a history of childhood physical and sexual abuse sought treatment for sexual identity issues. Married and divorced twice, this woman had several homosexual liaisons. One issue that emerged in therapy concerned her relationship with her fourteen-year-old daughter who abused chemicals, was frequently truant from school and acted out sexually through a number of affairs with men in their twenties and thirties. Shelly and her daughter were very close, slept in the same bed, bathed together, and shared the intimate details about various sexual encounters. Shelly shaved the girl's legs and pubic hair. In therapy, mother and daughter often sat with their legs entwined.

Forward refers to situations similar to those described above as "pseudo-incestuous," and notes that the resultant psychological harm often is as damaging as that in openly incestuous homes.[26] These two women derived secondary gains through the sexual misuse of their children. Under the guise of nurturing and affectionate parenting these pseudo-incestuous mothers were able to satisfy homosexual impulses.

Homosexual Pedophilia

When a man sexually abuses a child, he is commonly characterized either as a regressed or fixated pedophile.[27] Similarly, female molesters may be either regressed or fixated, homosexual or heterosexuals.

The regressed offender's sexual orientation is directed toward hetero or homosexual peers. Under stress, this individual often regresses or reverts to earlier modes of (fantasized) sexual gratification and molests a child or children. The offender often appears to be amenable to therapeutic interventions because the problem essentially involves temporary or transient regression.

On the other hand, the fixated pedophile has a decided sexual preference for children of either or both sexes, usually in specific age groups such as boys, aged nine-to-twelve, or girls, aged six-to-eleven. These individuals are both difficult to identify and to treat.

Until recently, the fixated pedophile was stereotyped as a lonely, socially-isolated single man between twenty and forty, who sought employment in positions that increased his proximity to children. Authorities now know that pedophiles are both male and female, heterosexual and homosexual, married or single and from every socio-economic group. They lead lives characterized by denial and they avoid detection with remarkable skill.

For example, a single female sex offender in her mid-thirties had sexually abused her three sons when they were between the ages of five and eight. In addition, she ran an unlicensed daycare facility from her home and was suspected of molesting countless other youngsters in her care. In a slightly different scenario, another woman, also the operator of a home daycare/babysitting service, served as a pimp for her pedophilic spouse, who molested twenty-two identified two- to three-year-old male children over a period of five years.

Finkelhor and Williams found that five percent of girls and twenty percent of boys were sexually abused by women, and that forty percent of daycare abuse was perpetrated by females.[28] Most female daycare abusers are in their thirties, married, mothers, have no criminal histories, use co-perpetrators to molest, and abuse females. In general, female perpetrators who act alone choose younger victims and engage in serious sex offenses. Sometimes force, mass abuse and ritualistic acts are involved.

Finkelhor and Williams present a typology of female daycare abusers which includes the lone woman who is the least common type, who denies molestation and who suffers from serious psychopathology such as multiple personality; the initiator who uses a partner and may be involved in child pornography; and the follower who is lonely and dependent and plays a subordinate role to her male co-partner.[29]

Mother Search

Some female molesters unconsciously appear to seek the warmth and nurturing of a mother when they sexually abuse their daughters. Often these women were molested as children.[30] As a result, they experienced inadequate parenting as children. Many were neglected and emotionally abandoned by mothers who sometimes sacrificed them to incestuous abuse. As adults, these women did not know how to parent. Justice notes that both incestuous fathers and collusive mothers are seeking the all-loving mother.[31]

These women often become incestuous themselves in order to satisfy dependency needs and needs for nurturance, closeness, intimacy and maternal gratification. Relationships are sexualized and roles are reversed.

In these families, either parent, or both, may sexually abuse the children. The nonoffending parent becomes the collusive partner, silently condoning family dysfunction and aberrations. One woman who molested (vaginal fondling, digital penetration and cunnilingus) her twelve-year-old daughter for six months, was not charged with the offense since the child recanted shortly after the initial disclosure. The girl, however, was placed in long-term foster care by a child protective services agency.

By mutual consent, there were no visits between the mother and daughter, although letters were exchanged. A portion of one of Mom's letters, intercepted by the child protective services caseworker, is excerpted below:

> "... So you see how sorry I am about all this. I know
> you blame yourself because I know how much you
> love me. You were always such a good daughter
> and you went through so much for me. You
> protected me first from Ron (biological father who
> beat both Mom and daughter) and then from Steve.
> I miss your caring and I appreciated all the things
> you did for me. I feel very blessed that you are my

daughter. And most of all I miss the way you worried about me and made sure that I was OK."

This parent wrote to her daughter as a child might well have written to Mother. The dynamic involved role reversal with a quest for nurturance from the child by the parent. In addition, the mother sexualized the relationship and culminated her search for nurturance by molesting her daughter.

Co-offender Selection

As noted earlier, a large percentage of female homosexual molestation appears to involve a partnership between a male and a female, or a male accomplice who aids in perpetrating the abuse.[32] Sometimes the woman is coerced or bribed into abusing the victim while her male partner derives sexual pleasure from watching the abuse, often masturbating while it is occurring. At other times, the man may participate actively in the deviant acts. The following case summary illustrates the dynamic of partner-accomplice abuse.

Bill sexually abused his fourteen-year-old daughter, Sarah, for two years with forced vaginal, anal and oral intercourse. Usually he abused the girl during the night in her bed after Mom was asleep. On a number of occasions, however, Sarah was told to join her parents in their bed, lying between the mother and father. Dad then would encourage or force Mom to sexually abuse Sarah. For example, a common scenario involved forced digital penetration by Mom while Dad watched and masturbated.

In some cases involving a male accomplice or partner, the man often may select the victim, usually a girl. When this occurs the mother may be involved in the homosexual molestation of a female child through her partner's choice rather than her own.

Notes: Chapter Two

1. Groth, A.N., 1981, 188-91. It is an error to assume that incestuous abuse is nonviolent. Current statistics do not separate aggressive from nonaggressive incest offenders.

2. Groth, A.N., 1981, 188-91.

3. Marvasti, J., 1986, 68.

4. Brown, M.E.; Hull, L.A.; and Panesis, S.K., October 12, 1984, 3-9.

5. While incestuous women often do not appear to have needs related to power, many of them are, at least partially, motivated by a need to dominate and control. Female rapists, however, often are overtly angry women whose behavior is motivated by rage and a desire to humiliate, hurt and overpower.

6. Backhouse, C., and Cohen, L., 1981, 144-48.

7. Similar to Rape Trauma Syndrome, the Sexual Harassment Syndrome includes symptoms such as a decline in work performance, internalized guilt and self-blame, depression, psychogenic problems (stomachaches, headaches, nausea, involuntary muscle spasms, hypertension) and in some cases, psychological breakdown.

8. McCarty, 1987, 447-57.

9. One theory attributed the high percentage of homosexual molestation among female offenders to the participation of male accomplices. Men generally select female victims. However, the high incidence of homosexual molestation among female offenders who abuse independently refutes this theory.

10. This finding refutes the theory that sibling incest is relatively harmless.

11. Herman, J., 1981, 18.

12. When considering mother-son rape, it is important to document the circumstances of the assault. For example, one male sex offender in therapy reported that at age fifteen, he had "molested" his mother by entering her bedroom and fondling her vagina several nights per week for over a year. Never once did it occur to this man that his mother allowed the abuse to continue.

13. Haugaard, J.J., and Reppucci, N.D., 1988, 128.

14. Forward, S. and Buck, C., 1979, 73-82.

15. Haugaard, J.J. and Reppucci, N.D., 1988.

16. Justice, B., and Justice, R., 1979, 193.

17. Groth, A.N., 1981, 190-91.

18. Forward, S. and Buck, C., 1979, 117-24.

19. Russell, O.E.H. (Ed.), 1984.

20. Forward, S., and Buck, C., 1979, 117-24.

21. Abusers actively violate children. They are motivated by an unconscious need to re-enact early trauma in their own lives; or they either identify with the aggressor (who abused them) or displace anger from childhood trauma. By contrast, colluders operate covertly. They enable, encourage or passively allow the abuse to occur. Their motives vary. Some colluders unconsciously allow abuse to keep their marriages together and maintain the status quo. Others allow abuse as a "pay back" for the child. The adult may be jealous of their spouse's fondness for the child or they

want their child to suffer by experiencing trauma similar to their childhood suffering.   Still others vicariously relive their own childhood trauma when their offspring are molested.

22.   McCarty, 1987, 56-57.

23.   Brown, M.E.; Hull, L.A.; and Panesis, S.K., October 12, 1984, 3-9.

24.   Wolfe, F.A., March 1985, 1-8.

25.   Marvasti, J., 1986, 67.

26.   Forward, S. and Buck, C., 1979.

27.   Groth, A.N., 1981.

28.   Finkelhor, D., and Williams, L.M., 1988.

29.   Finkelhor, D., and Williams, L.M., 1988, 45-50.

30.   Wolfe, F.A., March, 1985, 1-8; and McCarty, 1986, 447-58.

31.   Justice, B. and Justice, R., 1979, 147.

32.   Wolfe, F.A., 1985, 1-8.   Fifty percent of the offenders in Wolfe's sample of female perpetrators had male partners or accomplices. Wolfe described these women as socially isolated and prone to use the defense mechanisms of dependence, denial, rationalization and projection.

3
CAUSES

No single theory accounts for all cases of female molestation. However, several patterns suggest common elements among some perpetrators.

RE-ENACTMENT OF EARLY TRAUMA[1]

One explanation for child molestation relates to early victimization of the offender. Statistics from various studies indicate that fifty to eighty percent of adult male sex offenders were molested as children. In an (unsuccessful) attempt to master childhood trauma, the victim may identify with the aggressor (i.e., the person who abused him or her) and become a teenaged or adult offender. As an offender, this person repeatedly re-enacts his or her own abuse in an unconscious and futile attempt to master the unresolved trauma. The victim becomes the victimizer. Even though the trauma is not resolved, the victim regains power and control through perpetration.

Sometimes, victims of sexual aggression displace anger at the perpetrator onto helpless and powerless children whom they then abuse. Through perpetration, these former victims find a release for the suppressed rage they harbor at their own abusers.

Displaced anger and identification with the aggressor are common sequelae for both male and female child victims of sexual abuse, and they have been identified as causative factors for female sex offenses.[2] Marvasti, who subscribes to the theory that identification with the aggressor is a causative factor in female sex offenses, hypothesizes that female victims identify with their own mothers in their incestuous families of origin. Even though the father may have been the victimizer, the mother may be the perceived aggressor since her abandonment and rejection of her child has been active and intense.[3]

SADISTIC CRIMINAL BEHAVIOR

De River,[4] describes the female sadistic criminal who often uses a lover to carry out violent sexual crimes. This type of sex offender is extremely rare. Antipathy toward people who have abused these women motivates criminal acts which can be premeditated or impulsive. Blame is projected onto accomplices and offenses are minimized. Motivated by revenge, power needs, hatred and jealousy, and lacking in maternal feelings, these women appear to be either severely character disordered or psychotic. They resemble males who engage in sadistic sexual offenses.

While symptomatology as extreme as that manifested by the violent sexual criminal is uncommon, it is seen in less severe degrees in some female sex offenders in treatment. Women characterized by polymorphous perversity, physically abusive behaviors and indiscriminate victim selection, and who subsequently deny or minimize offenses with an attitude of cold disdain, resemble to some extent the criminal psychopath.

In discussing female rape, Groth provides case examples that appear to fit the category of the sadistic criminal.[5] He notes that some cases of female rape involve sex-related homicide. One woman, for example, angry that her lover was going to leave her, drugged and castrated him. Another female sex offender burned her eight-year-old son's feet with hot water; kicked him in the testicles; grabbed, pulled, and yanked his penis; squeezed his testicles; and hit and jabbed him with broom handles. Groth does not label or classify these women. However, the dynamic clearly is different from that of a number of women molesters since it involves sexual cruelty and sadism.[6]

NARCISSISM

Forward describes the infantile, narcissistic and needy female sex offender who molests her daughter whom she perceives as an extension of herself. Forward describes these women as emotionally disturbed to the point of psychosis. Unable to nurture and in need of nuturance themselves, they reverse roles with their daughters who become martyrs in meeting their mothers' needs. Molestation often begins when the girls are very young. The offenses are described almost as masturbatory for self-stimulation and emotional feeding.[7]

The narcissistic type of offender suffers from a poor sense of self with blurred boundaries between self and others. Many of these mothers are impulsive, unpredictable, unstable, manipulative and self-centered with low frustration tolerance. Often there are manifestations of identity disturbance. Their personalities are marked by insecurity and uncertainty in areas of gender identity. With histories of self-defeating and self-destructive behaviors, both interpersonally and vocationally, they perpetually experience an inner emptiness, boredom and frustration.

A typical narcissistic offender was referred for therapy by her physician who felt that her sense of hopelessness, low self-esteem and psychogenic complaints related to unresolved early incestuous victimization. During her first session, the client almost boastfully disclosed that she placed pencils into her infant daughter's vagina while masturbating to climax. Although she was oriented to time and place and did not manifest auditory or visual hallucinations or delusions, this woman's affective responses were totally inappropriate. She lacked insight regarding her offenses. Her child was an extension of herself, an object or vehicle to be used for self-pleasure.

OBSERVATIONS

Due to the lack of empirical and clinical data of female sex offenders, conclusions regarding the causes of female sex offenders must be tentative and hypothetical. In addition, there is considerable overlap within and between categories. For example, the narcissistic offender can be, and sometimes is, a homosexual pedophile in search of a mother. In addition, narcissism and symbiosis are closely linked; some narcissistic offenders form symbiotic relationships with their daughters. Finally, understanding the reasons for female molestation is complicated by innumerable variables, by lack of sound studies and by complex interpersonal dynamics.

Nonetheless, we do know much more than we did just a few years ago. We believe, for example, that rape by females occurs along a continuum, starting with sexual harassment, motivated by rage and power needs. We know that the female rapist, like her male counterpart, is likely to be young, knows her victim, assaults in the home and is not likely to be convicted of the crime. Her victims, usually minors, suffer from a variety of symptoms identified as Rape Trauma Syndrome (RTS).

However, there is a definite need for more research studies focusing on demographics, incidence, frequency, typology, etiology and effective treatment modalities. Even more, data on mothers who sexually abuse their children is practically nonexistent. Society in general, and the criminal justice system in particular, virtually ignores this serious form of psychological and social pathology. The result of this denial is truly unfortunate, since victims of maternal sexual molestation often suffer from the most severe emotional consequences.

Notes: Chapter Three

1. Some of the dynamics involved in homosexual molestation, such as re-enactment of childhood trauma, apply equally to heterosexual molestation with either male or female perpetrators.

2. Marvasti, J., 1986, 64; Mathews, R., 1987.

3. Marvasti, J., 1986, 64.

4. De River, J.P., 1950, 160-77

5. Groth, A.N., 1981, 188-89.

6. Criminal sexual psychopathy may be manifest in some cases of daycare abuse involving ritualistic sadism.

7. Forward, S. and Buck, C., 1979, 117-18.

4

Effects on Victims

The effects of sexual abuse by female perpetrators vary in kind, degree and intensity depending upon the following:

- nature of abuse;

- frequency of acts;

- age at onset of abuse;

- use of coercion or threats;

- relationship with offender;

- victim's perception of abuse;

- responses of others to the abuse.

In general, victims of female perpetrators manifest symptoms similar to those experienced by victims of other types of molestation. These effects are documented in the literature and include a wide range of behavioral and emotional problems, such as:

- guilt and self-blame;

- depression;

- anxiety;

- interpersonal problems;

- suicidality;

- dissociation;

- sexual dysfunction (difficulties becoming aroused, vaginismus, etc.);

- PTSD (Post Traumatic Stress Disorder);

- low self-esteem;

- ambivalence;

- confusion of sex with love/intimacy;

- regression;

- poor parenting skills;

- inability to trust;

- antisocial behavior (such as stealing, truancy, or runaway)

- promiscuity, sexual inhibition or confusion about (sex) norms and standards.

INTERACTION WITH OTHERS

Lists of symptoms tell us little about how victims relate to others. Victims who were molested by female offenders tend to exhibit the following patterns in their relationships with others. They may:

● victimize others;

● experience confusion about their gender role;

● allow abuse to occur within their family; and,

● be victimized by nonfamily members.

Victimizing Others

Some authorities note that molested women victimize children at higher rates than those who were never molested. Groth reports that sixty percent of his sample of male sex offenders were victimized as children; twenty percent of these offenders were victimized by women.[1] Finkelhor cites sexual preoccupation and sexualization of relationships as effects of victimization (i.e., as part of the "traumagenic" dynamic associated with the abuse cycle).[2]

Gender Confusion

With female homosexual molestation, psychosexual issues and sexual identity confusion are common and often are compounded by betrayal issues. Mothers especially are expected to protect and nurture their children, not molest them. Homophobia and fear of homosexuality are generated by homosexual molestation.

Victims of same-sex molestation often feel isolated and different. They may experience an unhealthy (symbiotic), enmeshed interdependence with the perpetrators. For example, the deep attachment and bond between the adult male pedophile and his male child victim has been thoroughly documented in the literature. Similarly, daughters molested by their mothers often are attached to the offending parent with blurred and confused ego boundaries and a poor sense of self.

In-home Molestation

Victims of female incest offenders typically are found enmeshed in families that are socially isolated and interdependent. Also, role reversals between parents and children are common. Furthermore, trust and betrayal issues compound the effects of molestation.

Out-of-home Molestation

Out-of-home molestation is no longer confined to the adult male perpetrator who preys upon lonely children. Women have been identified as pedophiles with victims as young as six months of age. Often there are sadistic, ritualistic elements as seen in a number of highly-publicized daycare settings in recent years. Victims of sadistic abuse usually are severely traumatized with generalized fears and very poor reality contact.

FEMALE VERSUS MALE PERPETRATORS[3]

Recent studies have been contradictory regarding the effects of female versus male molesters. Theories of causation are nonexistent or hypothetical, generally lacking in supportive data.

Johnson and Shrier studied eleven male adolescents victimized by women. They found that women molesters of male victims occurred with greater frequency than had been previously known. In the overall sample of five hundred, eleven victims of females were identified in contrast to fourteen male victims of men. Victims of both men and women experienced trauma and were at high risk of sexual dysfunction. Three quarters of the offenders attempted to get their victims to ejaculate. Multiple acts of abuse were common. In general, the women perpetrators used persuasion and not force.[4]

Finkelhor and Russell[5] found that adults molested as children rate experiences with male perpetrators as more traumatic than those with female perpetrators. If victims perceive abuse by females as somewhat less traumatic, then they are less likely to disclose acts that might result in the criminal prosecution of the perpetrator. Johns and Shier also found that the sexual abuse of boys by women is less likely to affect adolescent sexual identity than is the sexual abuse by males.[6] On the other hand, Marvasti notes that in five documented cases of mother-son incest, the mothers or sons were psychologically disturbed and possibly psychotic. In three documented cases of mother-daughter incest, the daughters became schizophrenic.[7]

The tendency to minimize the impact of female molesters may relate to two conditions. First, women are perceived as nonthreatening physically. Second, women in general are not as genitally-focused as are males. Society permits women to engage in a variety of touching behaviors, some of which may be sexually stimulating. These behaviors, however, can be rationalized as nonsexual and harmless.

Some victims may not give significance to female perpetration and yet they experience severe psychological damage.[8] For example, victims suffering from Borderline Personality Disorder often are not able to clearly identify symptomatology.

Lew is one of the few authorities to focus attention on male victims. Mother molestation, which is particularly traumatic due to cultural expectations related to trust and bonding, often results in fully repressed memories. Sometimes the first partially occluded memories do not surface until the victim is an adult.

Lew discusses the confusion and sense of isolation experienced by boys who are sexually abused by older women. Society romanticizes and minimizes the impact female molesters have on their young male victims. If a boy discloses abuse, he may not be believed. If he physically enjoyed the molestation, he does not perceive himself as a victim, despite the fact that he may be suffering from the effects of abuse. Many will even suggest that he *should* have enjoyed the experience. If he did not enjoy aspects of the abuse, he may fear that he is homosexual. Either way, the young male victim of the older female is placed in an untenable situation.[9]

Victims of Mother-Son Incest

Forward examined mother-son and mother-daughter incest. She noted that mother-son incest has been treated lightly in the literature, Forward stresses the complicated dynamics, severe psychological repercussions and subtle trauma that result from a mother's violation of her male child. Ninety-five percent of the cases involve absent fathers with weak, dependent mothers. Forward suggests that the mothers are seeking substitutes for their spouses. In these families, the son becomes both a replacement for, and rival of, the father. As such, the son experiences a wide range of damaging emotions (guilt, desire, love and hate) that result in identity problems later in life. Many of the boys eventually become homosexuals; some become rapists and murderers. Others suffer from sexual dysfunctions such as impotence.[10]

According to Forward, mother-daughter incest is rare and poorly understood. It often involves an emotionally disturbed mother who perceives her daughter as an extension of herself. The daughter becomes a martyr whose function is to satisfy her mother's needs. Roles are reversed with the child nurturing the infantile and needy mother.

At this point, however, there has been too little systematic study of these victims to fully understand all of their characteristics. Yet we can say this: being victimized by sexual assault, whether by a male or a female perpetrator, usually results in long-term adjustment problems for the victim.

A Victim Speaks

"By age three, I hated my mother. I was her third child under age six and her oldest daughter. I wasn't wanted...My parents were very religious and they didn't drink at all. They met each other in grade school and were best friends and got engaged early. My mother was sixteen and my father was eighteen when they got married. Dad really depended on the relationship, and I think that he closed his eyes to a lot that went on. His mother had died when he was three and his father just took off, so my father was raised by his grandparents and I think he missed out on a lot of love.

"I believe that my mother sexually abused all of us kids. I know for sure that she beat us. Dad must have known about it, especially when she used a 'two by four' board on us. The last time she hit me was when I was fourteen and I hit her back. She never touched me again after that. And Mom slept around a lot, too. Dad acted as if she didn't, but in a little Texas town, everybody knew about her.

"Talking about the molestation is hard. It's still very painful and I didn't remember it for a long time. I still don't remember all of it, and I'm thirty-six. One of my earliest memories is walking upstairs at home with my mother grabbing my butt from behind. I used to stumble up the stairs just to get away from her. I also have flashes of her shoving things up my vagina. I remember her fingering me a lot. I can't remember being forced to do anything to her. She always did things to me. I slept in her bed between age one and five. I have a recurring memory of staring at a spot on the wall when I was in bed with her. The spot was like a big ball with funny shapes inside of it. It got bigger and bigger as I stared at it and it would roll toward me. Finally it would just roll over me. I don't really know but I may have been molested then."

The forty year old single woman who wrote the above account of mother molestation alluded to the passive, collusive role that her father played in the family dynamic. The role of the male silent partner parallels the collusive mother in father-daughter incestuous abuse. Weak, passive and dependent, these partners usually deny abuse, or worse, they subtly encourage its occurrence in order to pacify their spouses.

This female victim suffered from molestation by her mother. In her early teens, she sexually abused some of the male and female toddlers for whom she babysat. She remembered digitally penetrating several little girls and fondling the penises of young boys. As an adult, she still feared a recurrence of the impulse to molest children.

During adolescence, she was sexually promiscuous but stated that she enjoyed sex only "if I weren't present." Sex was "scary, dirty and shameful if I thought about it. How could I enjoy that?" Like the toddler staring at the wall to dissociate from a traumatic experience, this woman mentally escaped during periods of sexual intimacy. Engaged three times for brief periods, she was unable to sustain a relationship with a man, could not trust and did not understand how to "mix intimacy with sex." She made several suicide attempts. She also used alcohol and marijuana to ease the pain. The ultimate solution was to avoid sex altogether and become "asexual." At the time of her disclosure regarding the incestuous relationship with her mother, she had been celibate for five years.

Teenaged Female Molesters

Research with adult male sex offenders has resulted in increased knowledge regarding the juvenile male population. For example, a large percentage of adult male sex offenders were molested and physically abused as children, and they began to perpetrate sex offenses in their preteen years. Increased knowledge of juvenile male sex offenders has resulted in a proliferation of treatment programs for these adolescents.

It is only recently that clinicians have begun to gather and share information about offending females derived from client populations. A study of seventeen female adolescent victim-offenders in outpatient therapy in the Phoenix metropolitan area during 1985-88 resulted in interesting findings. The girls were referred to therapy because each one was a victim of incestuous abuse. Many of the teenagers were wards or dependents of the court in long-term foster care because they had been rejected or abandoned by the nonoffending parents who supported the perpetrators. A number of these youngsters manifested severe symptoms, including sexual promiscuity, delinquency, runaway behavior, truancy, suicidal attempts and chemical abuse.

What follows are brief summaries, including diagnoses, description of offenses and relevant history, for eight of the teenaged perpetrators whose profiles are typical of the entire sample.

Sally

Diagnosis: Histrionic Personality Disorder with dissociative features

Full Scale I.Q.: 102

Age and Circumstances of Disclosure: During group therapy for teenaged victims, at age fifteen.

Type of Offense: Genital fondling of nine-month old male; insertion of eyedropper into infant's rectum

Frequency and Duration of Offense: One occurrence disclosed

Age of Offender at Time of Perpetration: Twelve years

Relationship to Victim: Babysitter

Relevant History of Offender: Multiple sexual victimizations since infancy by various adult male perpetrators including biological and stepfather.

Legal consequences Following Disclosure: None

Mary

Diagnosis: Conduct Disorder

Full Scale I.Q.: 93

Age and Circumstances of Disclosure: During individual therapy at age thirteen

Type of Offense: Digital penetration, insertion of objects into vagina of two girls, aged five and seven

Frequency and Duration of Offense: Several occurrences during a six to eight month period of time.

Age of Offender at Time of Perpetration: Twelve years

Relationship to Victim(s): Half-sister

Relevant History of Offender: Long-term sexual abuse by stepfather from age six to twelve

Legal Consequences Following Disclosure: None

Betsy

Diagnosis: Borderline Personality Disorder, Learning Disabled

Full Scale I.Q.: 75

Age and Circumstances of Disclosure: During group therapy for teenaged victims at age fourteen

Type of Offense: Genital fondling of eight year old male

Frequency and Duration of Offense: One occurrence disclosed

Age of Offender at Time of Perpetration: Fourteen years

Relationship to Victim: Foster sibling

Relevant History of Offender: Multiple physical and sexual abuse by various adult male relatives since age three

Legal Consequences Following Disclosure: None

Jennie

Diagnosis: Developing Borderline Personality Disorder

Full Scale I.Q.: 84

Age and Circumstances of Disclosure: During individual therapy at age thirteen

Type of Offense: Genital fondling of two girls, aged four and six

Frequency and Duration of Offense: Several times weekly for nineteen months

Age of Offender at Time of Perpetration: Eleven years

Relationship to Victim(s): Half-sister

Relevant History of Offender: Multiple sexual victimizations since infancy by two stepfathers and one adult male family friend

Legal Consequences Following Disclosure: None

Felice

Diagnosis: Borderline Personality Disorder: Learning Disabled

Full Scale I.Q.: 75

Age and Circumstances of Disclosure: During group therapy for teenaged victims at age thirteen

Type of Offense: Genital fondling of eight-year-old male

Frequency and Duration of Offense: One occurrence disclosed

Age of Offender at Time of Perpetration: Fourteen years

Relationship to Victim: Foster sibling

Relevant History of Offender: Multiply physically and sexually abused by various adult male relatives since age three

Legal Consequences Following Disclosure: None

Jo-Lynn

Diagnosis: Conduct Disorder

Full Scale I.Q.: 100

Age and Circumstances of Disclosure: During individual therapy at age thirteen

Type of Offense: Breast and vaginal fondling of two girls, aged six and eight

Frequency and Duration of Offense: Three times during a one month period of time

Age of Offender at Time of Perpetration: Thirteen

Relationship to Victim(s): Foster sibling

Relevant History of Offender: Sexually abused by stepfather from age ten to thirteen

Legal Consequences Following Disclosure: None

Carrie

Diagnosis: Developing Borderline Personality Disorder; ADD (Attention Deficit Disorder)

Full Scale I.Q.: 76

Age and Circumstances of disclosure: During group therapy for teenaged victims at age fourteen

Type of Offense: Genital fondling of five year old male; genital fondling and cunnilingus with nine year old female

Frequency and Duration of Offense: Periodically over several months with each victim

Age of Offender at Time of Perpetration: Eleven years (male victim); twelve years (female victim)

Relationship to Victim: Half-brother; sister to girlfriend

Relevant History of Offender: Multiple sexual victimizations by adult males (boyfriends of mother) and teenaged and adult females (babysitters, aunts)

Legal Consequences Following Disclosures: None

Cara

Diagnosis: Developing Borderline Personality Disorder

Full Scale I.Q.: 79

Age and Circumstances of Disclosure: During individual therapy at age fifteen

Type of Offense: Genital fondling of six-year-old male

Frequency and Duration of Offense: Periodically over several months

Age of Offender at Time of Perpetration: Eleven years

Relationship to Victim: Neighbor

Relevant History of Offender: Sexually abused by biological father from age four to fifteen; raped by older brother at twelve; sibling incest at seven with eight-year-old sister; physical abuse by mother

Legal Consequences Following Disclosure: None

Findings

Reviewing the data for the entire sample of seventeen female sex offenders yielded the following information:

1. As with juvenile male offenders, many of the girls began committing sex offenses prior to adolescence, often with exploratory yet exploitative contact with younger children.

2. Only two of the girls were involved with co-partners (a boyfriend and a brother) during their offenses. In existing current samples, adult female molesters have high rates of involvement with male co-offenders.

3. Male and female juvenile sex offenders appear to share similar dysfunctional backgrounds, including a prevalence of physical, sexual and emotional abuse and neglect.

4. At least half of the girls had perpetrated homosexual offenses and several of the victims were very young children. Current data does not indicate that male adolescent offenders demonstrate a proclivity toward homosexual molestation. Studies do indicate, however, that adult female molesters have fairly high rates of homosexual molestation.

5. All of the teenaged girls knew their victims who were relatives, siblings, relatives of friends or neighbors or children for whom they babysat. Current data indicates that offenders of both sexes tend to know their victims.

6. In general, the girls manifested character problems (low frustration tolerance, objectification of others, manipulation, absence of guilt and remorse, and a need for immediate gratification). One of the teenagers was diagnosed as histrionic and half of the sample as developing Borderline Personality Disorder.

7. Unlike their male counterparts, the majority of the girls were low mental functioning. Over half had fullscale I.Q.'s under 85.

8. The teenaged female perpetrators disclosed in therapy often months or years after perpetration of the offenses. Many juvenile male offenders are reported to the police by victims or relatives soon after the offenses.

9. There were no legal consequences for the teenaged females who perpetrated the sex offenses.

Data from clinical samples is important to facilitate an understanding of the dynamics underlying offending behaviors. The data also is used to develop treatment strategies which may differ for female versus male offenders.

EFFECTS ON MALE VICTIMS

Sarrel and Masters (1982) note that the difference between male and female rape victims is that men do not feel guilty regarding the fact that they may have invited abuse.[11] However, according to Timnick, male victims, like their female counterparts, suffer from Rape Trauma Syndrome (RTS).[12] Sarrell and Masters (1982) found eleven cases of sexual assault by women where their male victims developed Rape Trauma Syndrome.[13] First identified by Burgess and Holmstrom in the early 1970's, RTS consists of a cluster of psychological, behavioral, and somatic symptoms that rape victims experience following sexual assault. The syndrome, similar to Post Traumatic Stress Disorder (PTSD), but specific to the rape experience, consists of an initial crisis phase followed by a readjustment period.

EARLY PREDICTOR INDICATORS

Young victim-perpetrators are becoming the focus of therapeutic interventions. This is based on the logical assumption that they are more amenable to treatment than adults since they have a shorter history of abusing behaviors and since these behaviors have not become compulsive or habitual.[14] In addition, without therapy, child perpetrators usually become adult offenders.[15]

Predicting which child victims might become adolescent or adult molesters is a difficult task even for discerning therapists. However, there are a number of high-risk indicators as highlighted in the following case histories involving three to six-year-old female victims in play therapy. These indicators include: early traumatization from molestation; persistent symptoms resulting from the trauma; extreme sexualization; and, onset of sexually assaultive or aggressive behavior.

Mary

Sexually abused from age one to two-and-one-half by adult male and female teachers in preschool, this child was told that she would go to jail if she disclosed. The abuse involved cunnilingus and insertion of objects into her rectum with resultant anal lax tone and wink reflex. By age three, Mary was hyperactive, belligerent, and enuretic. She was obsessed with fantasies of murder and mutilation. In addition, Mary was beginning to act out sexually. At four, she tried to french kiss male and female peers. At age five, she was caught trying to insert a small bar of soap into the rectum of a female friend. Having been educated regarding appropriate and inappropriate behaviors, she was afraid to come to therapy for fear that she would be arrested.

Shelly

This child was sexually abused by her biological father until age three. Abuse involved urologia, vaginal fondling and insertion of objects into the vagina. Resultant symptoms included compulsive drawing of naked figures with explicit genitalia, compulsive insertion of objects such as kleenex, crayons and small plastic toys into her own vagina, and sexual acting out with animals and children. On several occasions, Shelly was found in a closet fellating the family collie. She repeatedly would ask little boys to show her their penises as she lifted her skirt or pulled down her pants.

Amber

Molested from age eighteen months to three years, Amber identified her perpetrator as the husband of her adult baby-sitter, a man subsequently convicted of abusing over twenty infants and toddlers. Amber's symptoms involved compulsive masturbation, seductive behaviors with adult males and females, fear of the dark, nightmares, and encopresis. She and her three year old female friend were found naked on the bathroom floor humping and french kissing. Amber alleged that her friend initiated these behaviors.

Connie

This child was molested by her stepfather on several occasions at age two-to-two and one-half. Abuse consisted of fellatio, cunnilingus, and digital penetration. Resultant symptoms included nightmares, compulsive masturbation, use of sexually precocious language and constant allegations of being randomly molested by adults of both sexes. Connie attempted to engage in fellatio with a cousin who was four and she frequently tried to grab the crotches of little boys.

Michelle

Diagnosed paranoid schizophrenic, Michelle's biological father molested her from early infancy to age three with perverse acts of urologia and coprophilia. He coerced fellatio by telling the toddler that his penis was a baby bottle which she should suck. Michelle suffered from night terrors, chronic enuresis, clinging behaviors, fear of strangers and constipation. She tried to fellate the family poodle.

June

By age six, June was offering two-year-old male toddlers candy bars in exchange for sexual favors, (i.e., mutual masturbation). At first, she denied her perpetrating behaviors despite complaints from the parents of three toddlers who had witnessed the deviant acts. Finally, June admitted mutual fondling with the boys but alleged that she had not initiated the acts. Both of June's older sisters had been sexually abused by their stepfather. A compulsive masturbator and a fearful, hyperactive child diagnosed ADD (Attention Deficit Disorder), June had witnessed the rape of her ten-year-old sister by the stepfather. Subsequently, at age five, she was repeatedly masturbated by this sister.

Notes: Chapter Four

1. Groth, A.N., March 15, 1982.

2. Finkelhor, D., 1986. Unlike several authorities, Finkelhor believes that female molestation generally is less damaging than male abuse, possibly because the culture defines women as essentially powerless and nonthreatening. The author does note, however, that the impact depends on the degree of maternal impairment and that victims with impaired mother ties react worse to molestation than those with more solid parental bonds.

3. One interesting study of male and female victims of molestation (Briere, Evans, Duntz and Wall, 1988, 457-61), found no gender differences in long-term sequelae.

4. Johnson, R.L. and Shrier, D., 1987, 650-52.

5. Finkelhor, D., 1984,; Russell, D.E.H., 1986.

6. Johns, R.L. and Shier, D. K., May 22, 1985.

7. Marvasti, J., 1986, 63-69.

8. An example of denial involved a male sex offender in therapy. He persisted in denying having experienced any type of sexual abuse as a child. After sixteen months of therapy, however, he recounted innumerable incidents that occurred between his third and seventh year of age when his mother bathed him, playing a game called, "Search for the Soap."

    During each bath, the mother hid a bar of soap under her son's penis. In order to retrieve the soap, she fondled the boy's genitals.

    Members of this offender's therapy group helped him to understand that his mother was sexually provocative and inappropriate during these bathing incidents. As one group member asked, "How would the bathing games have been perceived had they been by an adult male with his five-year-old daughter?"

9. Lew, M., 1988, 83-85.

10. Forward, S. and Buck, C., 1979.

11. Sarrell, P.M., and Masters, W.H., 1982, 117-31.

12. Timnick, L., 9-83, 74.

13. Sarrell, P.M. and Masters, W.H., 1982, 117-31.

There do not appear to be any studies on adult females raped by female perpetrators. It is likely that these victims also suffer from Rape Trauma Syndrome.

14. In contrast to this logical assumption, some clinicians believe that victims identified as perpetrators as children are, in fact, not amenable to treatment because of the degree of pathology already manifesting itself in so young a population.

15. Perpetration by young children involves a differential related to both power/coercion and to experience. A five-year-old molested boy has knowledge and learned behaviors that his nonmolested peers do not have. In other words, his sexual acting-out behaviors are not based on normal curiosity and experimentation.

5
Treating Young Offenders

Each of the children described in Chapter 4 had engaged in serious sexual acting-out behaviors by age six. Traumatized by sometimes bizarre and perverse abuse, and highly sexualized during infancy, the children all experienced persistent symptoms as a result of molestation. In addition, each had begun to act out with sexually aggressive or assaultive behaviors. In the absence of supportive home environments and intense therapeutic interventions, there was a high likelihood that these children would become future perpetrators.[1]

Treatment for these children involved play therapy focusing on abuse and related issues such as fears, psychogenic manifestations, enuresis and acting-out behaviors. Behavioral management approaches were implemented to curb sexual acting out. Parents and caregivers were involved in the therapeutic process, particularly to facilitate institution of behavioral contingencies in the home.

In addition, a major focus of the therapy for the children involved structured activities designed to help each child learn that:

1. she should not let anyone touch her genitals nor should she touch anyone else's genitals;

2.   touching another child's genitals hurts that child;

3.   she can learn to avoid such touching by asking a parent or other
      trusted adult what to do, or by engaging in an alternative activity.

Each of these teachings were repeated in a variety of ways and presented as simple rules with easily understood contingencies. Alternate activities to molestation were specified on an individual basis for each child. Threats such as incarceration were not used in order to foster the likelihood of disclosures.

Notes: Chapter 5

1. Studies of female victims have shown inappropriate sexual behavior in child victims, including masturbation, excessive sexual curiosity, and frequent exposure of the genitals (Finkelhor, D., 1986, 151.). Untreated, many of these child victims continue to express inappropriate sexual behaviors that accelerate during the adolsecent and post-adolescent period.

6
Treating Women Offenders

The literature suggests few innovative approaches to the treatment of female sex offenders or victims of female abuse. Even among the burgeoning number of programs for adolescent offenders, there has been no attempt to isolate issues particular to the female population of abusers. Conspicuously absent are treatment issues related to the high incidence of homosexual molestation, co-offender collaboration, low intelligence among perpetrators-victims, and high incidence of (developing) Borderline Personality Disorder among perpetrators-victims. It is important to identify these issues in order to formulate treatment strategies.

CURRENT PROGRAMS

During 1986, the East Family Community Services Center in Maplewood, Minnesota, extended its Program for Healthy Adolescent Sexual Expression (PHASE) to include group, individual and family therapy for female adolescent offenders. Sixty females were adjudicated for sex offenses in Minnesota in 1986 and thirty to forty percent reported histories involving abuse, neglect and violence; physical and mental disorders; and early and extensive use of pornography.[1]

The PHASE program includes psychological assessments, sex education, and individual, family and group therapy. A two-hour intake is followed by eight weeks of education and assessment, including a two-hour weekly group, four individual therapy sessions and three to four family sessions. The six month treatment component includes weekly group and bi-weekly individual and family therapy.

The PHASE program is somewhat typical of the few existing treatment programs for female sex offenders. In general program elements include:

1. A lengthy and thorough intake process which includes psychological testing. Testing often employs the Minnesota Multiphasic Personality Inventory, and various sex inventories, projective techniques and intelligence testing;

2. An educational component teaching about healthy human sexuality;

3. Teaching about and providing exercises on stress management;

4. Family involvement when appropriate and feasible;

5. Group therapy with an emphasis on developing empathy for victims;

6. Helping clients to work through their history of victimization;

7. Individual sessions for implementation of behavioral management strategies to stop abusing behaviors, and;

8. Individual sessions to establish healthy avenues for meeting sexual and interpersonal needs.

The majority of existing programs for adolescent sex offenders attempt to intervene into abusing behaviors before they become patterned and habitual. Since most adolescent offenders also are victims of abuse, therapeutic interventions usually combine victim-offender issues.

Treatment interventions for individuals with Borderline Personality Disorder and low intelligence are, of necessity, superficial. For example, when challenged with Gestalt experiential techniques, these females often manifest shallow, emotionally confused, histrionic reactions. Sometimes, they withdraw, regress or dissociate.

Supportive and behavioral approaches appear to be most effective for reversing self-destructive behavior patterns. In addition, group therapy affords an environment of acceptance that helps improve self-esteem, enhances trust and facilitates disclosures. Many female victim-offenders experience extreme anxiety surrounding the issues of victimizing and victimization. Group therapy usually is helpful in alleviating these feelings which, in turn, results in lowered stress levels.

Like male offenders, the behavioral and emotional repertoire of most female perpetrators is quite limited. Reality therapy, environmental manipulation and behavioral management strategies can challenge self-defeating assumptions, open new avenues to counter depression and bring about improved coping strategies.

Physically, some female offenders seem to benefit from anti-depressant and anti-anxiety drugs during periods of stress. Unlike many male offenders who project and externalize issues, females tend to turn hostile impulses inward. Thus, their potential for suicide is high. In some instances, careful administration of medication may be required to counteract the risk of suicide through overdose. Finally, adjunctive support should be offered to female offenders through support groups that specialize in issues related to chemical abuse, spousal abuse, weight management and so forth.

In determining the most appropriate treatment for female offenders, a comparison with male sex offenders is helpful.

Male and Female Offenders

Similarities:

Male	Female
History of abuse	History of abuse
Low self-esteem	Low self-esteem
Exploitation of others	Exploitation of others
Lack of empathy	Lack of empathy
Lack of guilt and remorse	Lack of guilt and remorse
Identification with aggressor	Identification with aggressor
Socially inadequate	Socially inadequate
Sexualization of relations	Sexualization of relations
Objectification of others	Objectification of others
Ignorance regarding sex	Ignorance regarding sex

Differences:

Male	Female
Primary diagnosis; Antisocial Personality Disorder	Primary diagnosis: Border-line Personality Disorder
Power, control and displaced anger	Re-enactment of trauma
Eroticized anger	Absence of eroticized anger
Genital stimulation/release	Intimacy needs/need for nurturance
Fusion of sex and anger	Dissociation and compulsivity

Common Scenarios in Perpetration:

Male	Female
1. victim	1. victim
↓	↓
2. stress/anxiety	2. stress/anxiety
↓	↓
3. identification w/aggressor	3. dissociation to cope
	↓
	4. stimulus of child
↓	↓
4. stimulus of child	5. increased stress
↓	
5. increased stress	↓
↓	
6. release: aggressive acting out (molestation)	6. release: re-enactment of unresolved trauma in hope of mastery (molestation)

UNCONSCIOUS MESSAGES

The female offender's unconscious self-statements:

> "I did it. It's my fault I got molested. Therefore, I'm bad and I'll do it again to prove I'm bad. I'll molest someone." (self-blame for own abuse, identification with aggressor)

> "It didn't really happen to me. I wasn't molested. It was a dream (or it happened to someone else; I don't know what happened). I'm not aware of doing it to someone else." (dissociation, splitting)

The male offender's unconscious self-statements:

> "He did it to me. Therefore, I'm like him and will do it to someone else." (identification with aggressor)

> "He did it to me. I'm angry but I can't show it to him. I can release my anger by doing it to someone else." (displacement)

Consciously, female and male sex offenders often give themselves similar messages:

> "I need love. I need to feel cared about. She (victim) or he (victim) needs the same expression of love and caring that I need. We both want this to happen. We both will feel good when it does."

> "I need and deserve love. She (victim) or he (victim) can fulfill that need. No one will be hurt."

Both female and male offenders often deny the sexual aspects of molestation and claim consent. Men sometimes rationalize by denying more serious acts such as intercourse. They claim "love went too far" or say they simply were instructing their victims about sex.

For male molesters, anger management is an essential part of therapy. Both male and female offenders require interventions that focus on correcting erroneous thinking patterns, alleviation of guilt, self-image building and behavioral techniques for impulse control.

SUGGESTED THERAPY FOR
TREATABLE FEMALE MOLESTERS

Supportive

- to elicit disclosures through acceptance and trust-building;

- to alleviate stress via reassurance, validation and development of insight;

- to decrease isolation through befriending and group therapy;

- to break through blocking through ventilation, active

- listening, role plays and unsent letters to offenders;

- to improve self-image through acceptance and group support.

Behavioral-Environmental

- to redirect energies into positive, socially acceptable goals;

- to challenge erroneous assumptions about victimization and victimizing by facilitating an understanding of abuse, the abuse cycle and arousal patterns;

- to counter depression and anxiety by offering challenges to change and by broadening the offenders behavioral and emotional repertoire;

- to offer concrete relaxation and stress management techniques;

- to increase support structure through group therapy and referrals, and;

- to provide alternate behaviors for impulse control and situational issues that increase the likelihood of abuse.

Educational

- to provide training and information for improved social skills, communication and assertiveness, and;

- to provide factual information on sexuality and sex roles.

Medical

- to refer for psychiatric consultation for adjunctive medical support as needed.

Referrals

To provide specialized support from appropriate self-help groups such as Alcoholics Anonymous, Overeaters Anonymous, and so forth.

DO'S AND DON'TS

DO'S	DONT'S
Administer complete battery of psychological tests, including: WAIS (Wechsler Adult Intelligence Scale), MMPI (Minnesota Multiphasic	Assume that the client's stated history regarding victimizing behaviors or childhood traumas is accurate. Clients dissimulate and block, sometimes with

DO'S (Continued)

Personality Inventory), chemical abuse screening inventory, projective tests such as the TAT (Thematic Apperception Test), and Draw-a-Person or Draw-a-Family, personality inventories such as the 16PF, and sex inventories.[2]

Assume that accurate diagnosis may be difficult. Be aware of the possibility of MPD's (Multiple Personality Disorders) as a possible diagnosis.

Be extremely thorough during intake procedures. Have knowledge of symptoms commonly manifested by this client population including self-mutilation and eating disorders.

Take actions with reference to contact with minor children. Consult with probation and child protective agencies regarding the risk level posed by the client while in treatment. Any recommendation should place children's safety as the first priority.

DONT'S (Continued)

screen memories. Suggestible or histrionic clients sometimes "over-report" when fantasies of victimizing behaviors or past victimization become reality.

Preclude a team approach to treatment. Adjunctive group support, psychiatric consultations and coordination with probation officers, facilitate effective treatment.

Expect goals beyond the capacity of clients severely traumatized in childhood.

Become an enabler or co-dependent, a common trap for therapists working with clients who suffer from Borderline Personality Disorder.

DO'S (Continued)

Be nonjudgmental and sensitive
to the extreme difficulty
experienced by the client in
disclosing sex offenses and early
childhood trauma.

Avoid rapid confrontation and
catharsis for this fragile client
population with a high risk of
decompensation.

Avoid inducing symptom shift to
the possible detriment of the
client and others. Be aware of
underlying problems as well as
presenting symptoms.

DONT'S (Continued)

Mimic clients by minimizing,
rationalizing or denying
(severity of) offenses
committed.

Allow the client to
manipulatively "play the system"
system" by pitting therapists
against probation officers,
child protective services case-
workers, attorneys and so
forth.

Categorize by labeling
(homosexuality, pedophilia).
Sometimes aberrant sexual
behavior is symptomatic of
unidentified psychiatric disturbance rather than a
primary diagnosis.

Notes: Chapter Six

1.   Jackson, M., September 5, 1986.

2.   For male offenders, psychological testing usually is necessary and
     mandated by the courts and child protective agencies. Needed
     information sometimes can be obtained from partial or selective
     testing if court mandates are followed and if the diagnostic picture
     is clear, as in antisocial personalities. A number of jurisdictions
     now are mandating assessments and use of penile phallometers to
     measure arousal patterns in male offenders. A phallometer for
     women offenders exist but the device is not in common use.

7
TREATING VICTIMS OF WOMEN OFFENDERS

Many of the approaches and techniques developed to treat victims of male offenders are equally effective for use with children and adults who have been molested by females. Regardless of the sex of the perpetrator or his or her relationship to the victim(s), a number of the effects of sexual molestation are likely. The victims are likely to feel that they have been:

- betrayed;

- robbed of control over their bodies by the power of others;

- emotionally disarmed;

- shamed and embarrassed;

- made to live with secrecy and collusion;

- manipulated by coercion or threats;

- treated in an inhuman way; and

- caused to experience traumatic stress with an array of
  behavioral and emotional symptoms including fears,
  confusion, self-blame, guilt, acting-out behaviors,
  regression, enuresis, encopresis, nightmares,
  self-destructive acts, suicide, self-mutilation, eating
  disorders and so forth.

These and other similarities between victims (both male and
female) suggest that it is possible for victims of women to participate in
group therapy with victims of men; and why many of the same
behavioral and Gestalt approaches can be effective for symptom relief
and anger release. For example, role plays and letters to the offender on
the part of either males or females, may be effective for "letting go" of
abusive parents and for anger release.

One cautionary note, however, is in order. It may be
counterproductive for a child victim of female molestation to participate
in a group composed solely of victims of males since feelings of
alienation and difference often arise in such a setting. Child victims
need validation and a sense that they are not alone. In a group of
victims of males, the child may experience a sense of uniqueness (as a
victim of a woman) rather than the commonality of the abuse
experience.

DIFFERENCES IN EFFECTS

There are some important differences between victims of male
and female perpetrators and these differences should influence the
course of treatment. It is important, however, to realize that every
molestation is different, regardless of the sex of the perpetrator. Each
victim's experience is different depending on the relationship with the
perpetrator, age of child, type of abuse (duration, frequency, threats
used and acts committed), intelligence, general level of functioning,
adaptation skills, stressors and so forth.

There are three important differences for children molested by mothers and older females:

1. **Confusion.** Confusion is an anticipated result of any molestation. However, confusion takes on a different quality and is exacerbated when the perpetrator is female because of cultural expectations. Women and mothers are expected to bond, protect and empathize with children. They are "supposed to be trustworthy."

2. **Homosexuality.** This issue arises in any same-sex molestation. Female children molested by women, like boys molested by men, are vulnerable to sexual identity problems, homophobia and fear of homosexuality.

3. **Role Problems.** Again, because of cultural expectations and also because of the characteristics of many female molesters,[1] child victims often learn to perceive themselves as consenting participants or as offenders.

The trauma of molestation, compounded by problems such as those noted above, can result in the possibility of Multiple Personality Disorder (MPD) or Borderline Personality Disorder. To cope, the molested child may unconsciously separate him or herself from the traumatic experience and resultant sense of badness. Unconsciously, the message may be, "This is not happening to me...it is happening to her" (the other, bad self).

Because of the potential severity of problems resulting from female molestation, it is imperative that therapy begin as early as possible with the following needs addressed:

1. **Role Modeling.** The child needs a trusted adult who is consistent, honest and "there" for her or him.

2. **Behavioral Controls.** Confused, afraid and hurt, the child may feel "out of control" and have difficulty distinguishing between what is normal and not normal, and what is real and what is fantasy. The therapist must establish firm and consistent

behavioral controls in order to help the child more clearly recognize what is real.

3. **Alternate Avenues to Coping.** Alternate behaviors must be established to help the child cope with stress, acting-out behaviors and internal turmoil. Explanations that an offending mother is not a "bad" person but that she has problems may help the child begin to perceive others (including him or herself) less judgmentally. Suggestions for socially acceptable outlets for anger may help the child learn that it is permissible to experience negative emotions and to find appropriate ways to express these feelings.

4. **Clarification and Reflection.**[2] The child needs acceptance and attentive listening in a permissive setting where feelings can be labeled and behaviors explained.

5. **Reality Testing.** Reality testing should include permission to feel and think thoughts that society labels unacceptable without acting on such thoughts. Wanting to kill one's perpetrator is different from the act of murder. Drawing the perpetrator and destroying that drawing does not hurt anyone.

6. **"Letting Go" of Hurt.** Anger often masks overwhelming hurt in a molested child. Allowing the hurt to be expressed is a painful and difficult process that victims consciously and unconsciously try to avoid. However, there can be no resolution or completion unless underlying feelings are confronted and processed. Play and art therapy,[3] modalities that by-pass defenses for direct expression, are helpful in affective work along with Gestalt exercises.[4]

7. **Assertiveness.**[5] Like all victims, the child needs to begin to feel empowered and in control of his or her own body. He or she must be able to distinguish between protective and abusive adults and to set limits on adult behaviors by saying, "no," when rights are violated.

8. **Age-Appropriateness.** During abuse, growing youngsters are robbed of childhood. Part of the therapeutic process involves recovery of that lost childhood. Seductive behaviors, age inappropriate mannerisms and clothing, and pseudo-sophistication should be confronted directly but not judgmentally.

9. **Sexual versus Nonsexual Love.** The tendency to sexualize relationships is a typical effect of molestation. Through role modeling, role plays, and verbal explanations, the therapist may help a child understand the distinction between the different kinds and manifestations of love and the inappropriateness of sexual love in childhood.

10. **Coping With Loss.** The child who is victimized by a parent, friend or other role model may need to separate from that person. Even if the separation is only psychological or temporary, the quality of the relationship will change following disclosure. Usually grief results. The grieving process will involve denial, anger, bargaining, depression and acceptance. The child will need support, clarification and understanding through each stage.[6]

These ten needs which also characterize all victims of abuse, are particularly relevant to victims of female perpetrators, both qualitatively and quantitatively. The problems for such victims are especially severe. In many cases, most of these needs will be experienced simultaneously. Thus, the task of the therapist is difficult and stressful. Clinicians who treat this population should be experienced and knowledgeable about child molestation by both male and female offenders.

THERAPEUTIC TECHNIQUES

The following list of suggested techniques is geared for abused children. Many of the exercises, however, can be modified to use with the adult population. Group support, role plays, ventilation and sharing are helpful to victims of all ages. With children, parent involvement through dyad therapy, family sessions or consultations, is advisable whenever possible.

1. To help integrate the "good" and "bad" self that the victim
    experiences, first use Gestalt techniques to identify the different
    parts. Instructions are:

    ● Write or draw the good and bad "you" (Write or draw
      your good and bad self).

    ● Use colors or shapes to show the different parts of
      yourself.

Alter ego exercises also are helpful in identifying different aspects
of self. The child is asked to describe her "bad" self. The therapist,
standing behind her, then describes the child's "good" self.

As part of the integration process, such children may be asked to:

    ● Make a large circle and place their good and bad selves
      inside it. "What are the two selves saying to each
      other?" Other questions focus on, "Where are they
      located in the circle? How are they related to each other?
      Which self is bigger? Which is more important? How do
      they feel about each other? How would you feel if one
      were destroyed? If both were destroyed? Can they fit
      together? How?"

    ● Have the children write down or audiotape a dialogue
      (conversation) between their good and bad parts.
      "Which one said the most? Which one felt most like
      you?" (Interactive dialoging with use of puppets is
      effective with young children where the therapist plays
      the role of "good" self, while the child assumes the role of
      "bad" self.)

    ● Have the children make clay representations of their
      good and their bad selves. Let the tabletop (piece of
      newsprint, top of box) be the whole self. Have them
      place their good and bad self on the table top where they

think they belong. Ask: "Can they touch? Hug? Come together? Squish them together. How does that feel?"

- Ask the child to think of three ways he could help his good and bad selves be friends and live together inside him.

- After victims complete exercises such as the above, have them write a page about their good and bad selves and what they have learned about them.

2. To work through anger and feelings about their abusers, the children may write (unsent) letters describing the abusive acts, expressing their feelings and saying what they would like to see happen to their abusers. Incomplete sentence blanks such as the one that follows may elicit strong emotions:

- A mom who abuses is...

- And she is also...

- If I could say anything to Mom, it would be...

- What a Mom is...

- What a Mom does...

- The animal that looks like my anger is...

- The animal that looks like my hurt is...

- The animal that looks like my Mom is...

- The animal that looks like me is...

- The little girl in me says...

- Mommy, I need...

- And I also need...

- And I also want...

- I love Mommy and I also...

- If my hurt could talk it would say...

- If my anger could talk it would say...

- I am like my Mom because...

- I was abused and now I...

- The way I am like other people is...

- The way I am different from other people is...

- Sometimes I want to scream out...

3. To teach assertiveness, one may help victims to distinguish between their passive, aggressive and assertive behaviors and responses. Practice situations for role plays may be helpful in this regard. Examples are:

    - Asking your teacher for an extension on a class assignment

    - Telling your mother why you should not be grounded even though you did not do your chores for a week

    - Asking your father to stop spanking you as a punishment

    Some important needs related to assertiveness are:

- The need for appropriate nonverbal, as well as verbal, behaviors. (Nonverbal behaviors include direct eye contact, erect posture, feet solidly on the ground and so forth.)

- The need for contracting with self or others to accomplish certain goals. Assertively begin with the least threatening goals.

- The need to assertively request one's desires or perceptions (i.e., describe the situation as it is; express feelings about it; specify a desired change; and explain the consequence). For example, an assertive request is: "Mr. Jones, you have touched my leg twice today when helping me with class work (the situation). I feel very uncomfortable when you do that (feeling). Please don't touch my leg again (change requested)." Then things will be back to normal (consequence).

4. To help distinguish between behaviors that are normal and those that are not, and between fact and fantasy, the therapist may use both reality testing and role modeling. For example, one may set up situations involving logical consequences for mental processing such as:

- What is going on inside a Dad who leaves his daughter alone with her Mom when he knows she has been molested by her?

- What kind of father would do that?

- What would you do if your son or daughter were molested by your husband or wife?

- What do you think of a Mom who wants to sleep naked with, and hug, her eight-year-old daughter every night?

- Would you do that?

- Why not?

5.   The therapists also may need to instruct children on socially
     acceptable coping strategies and anger outlets. For example, use
     alternate story-telling and "brainstorming:"

     - Ask the children to recount a scary dream and then
       repeat the dream as recounted but change the ending.
       For example, the bad man or monster enters the house
       but, unlike in the original dream, he does not kill the
       child. The child is able to get to the phone and call 911.
       The police come and arrest the bad man.

     - Ask the children to say "no" in as many different ways
       as possible. Explain that there are just as many ways to
       solve a problem as there are to say "no." Then, together,
       "brainstorm" (and write down) all the ways to let out
       anger. Divide the list into three parts—the acceptable,
       nonacceptable and child's preferences (among the
       acceptable ways). A sample list would include: hitting,
       killing, punching (all unacceptable); pillow-pounding,
       playing football, shouting in the shower (acceptable); and
       pillow-pounding (preference).

6.   To help the children change any patterns of seductiveness one may
     use an individualized list of goals, objectives and methods.
     Children who act seductively may appear pseudo-sophisticated and
     need guidance on dress and mannerisms. Mirroring and role plays
     are usually effective, with the therapist playing the role of the
     child, to demonstrate traits that should be modified.[7]

7.   Sexually acting out children need to develop victim empathy to
     curtail their own abusive behaviors. Dyad work with another child
     victim often enhances identification which is a precursor to
     empathy. In some cases, asking a police officer from the sexual
     assault unit to talk with a child about the logical consequences of

sexually abusive behavior may help to modify aggression before it manifests itself in undesirable ways.

8.   To work through the grieving process with children who have been separated or severed from their abuser, the following techniques may be helpful:

   •   Instruct them to compile a book of memories including letters, photographs and mementos. Use the book as a catalyst for sharing in sessions. Give the children permission to vent both positive and negative feelings orally in sessions or in their journal writing.

   •   Encourage them to write letters (usually unsent) to the abuser, culminating in a final good-bye letter.

   •   Facilitate role plays to help them complete what they feel is unfinished business with their abusers.

9.   To clarify sexual feelings and relieve guilt and confusion related to homophobia and fear of homosexuality, the therapist may use an educationally permissive approach. Basic sexual education appropriate to the child's age and developmental stage may also clarify misconceptions concerning their bodies, abuse versus loving sexual relations, and the inappropriateness of sexual contacts for young children. Pre-adolescent and older children and teenagers usually require appropriate modeling and a nonjudgmental approach to their sexual preferences.

If the children have acted out sexually with a same sex peer or if they fear homosexuality, the best approach is to verbally seek to alleviate their guilt and self-doubt in a reassuring manner. Stress that they were victimized and were not consenting partners during molestation. Emphasize the difference between the body and mind. The body might respond to being touched, while the mind abhors the acts being perpetrated. Such children will be judging themselves. Any judgments, admonitions or moral strictures by the therapist will increase their feelings of guilt and self-doubt. It is best not to label or permit the children to label themselves as guilty. Stress to them that they are developing as human beings who have ample time for self-discovery.

These techniques may help you help children to focus on some of the major problems confronting them. What distinguishes the needs of victims of women from those who are victims of men is heightened confusion about sexual identity, reality, loss and integration of self. Hence, the emphasis in therapy should be on these problems which, along with all the other problems they face as victims of abuse in general are exacerbated for child victims of female perpetrators.

Notes: Chapter Seven

1. Female offenders often are seductive and in need of nurturance. Force and coercion usually are not used during molestation.

2. For an elaboration on the supportive, "Rogerian" approach to therapy, refer to the works of Carl Rogers. An excellent summary of client-focused therapy can be found in: Rogers, C., "Significant Aspects of Client-Centered Therapy", in (Ed.): *Varieties Of Personality Theory*. New York: E.P. Dutton & Co., Inc., 1964, 167-84.

3. Two excellent sources of play therapy are the classic work of Axline: Axline, V., *Play Therapy*. N.Y.: Houghton-Mifflin Co., 1947; and Schaeffer, C.E., & O'Connor, K.J. (Eds.) *Handbook Of Play Therapy*. N.Y.: John Wiley & Sons, 1983.

4. There are numerous sources on Gestalt therapy and techniques, among them: Fajan, J. & Shepherd, I.L. (Eds). *Gestalt Therapy Now: Theory, Techniques And Applications*. N.Y.: Harper Colophon, 1971; and Rhyne, J., *The Gestalt Art Experience*. Chicago, IL: Magnolia Street Publishers, 1984.

5. One of the best sources providing a comprehensive overview of assertiveness training is: Bower, S.A. and Bower, G.H. *Asserting Yourself: a Practical Guide For Positive Change*. Reading, MA: Addison-Wesley Pub. Co., 1976.

6. The stages that people experience when grieving are elaborated in: Kubler-Ross, E. *On Death And Dying*. N.Y.: MacMillan, 1969.

7. Transactional Analysis (T.A.) may also be helpful for teaching victims about the roles of adults and children, their interactions and the internalized adult-child in everyone.

GLOSSARY

alter ego - unconscious aspects of the self. In therapy, the clinician acts as the alter ego by voicing the client's unconscious feelings, guilts, wishes and unacceptable thoughts.

antisocial personality - a personality disorder characterized by absence of guilt and remorse, impulsivity, self-centeredness, expedience, manipulation, inability to self-correct, low frustration tolerance, exploitation, and objectification of others, denial of responsibility for personal acts and conflict with authority.

behaviorism - therapeutic approach based on learning theory; focuses on observable antecedents and consequences of behaviors.

boundaries - functional boundaries (differentiations) between external and internal, fantasy and reality, self and others; prerequisite to mental health. Boundaries dissolve in schizophrenia when patients report anxiety over loss of identity.

catharsis - the reliving of past trauma in therapy through moments of conscious recall with accompanying release of feelings; also called abreaction.

character disorder - personality trait and pattern disturbance describing characteristics associated with criminals (absence of guilt and remorse, impulsivity, expedience, manipulation and so forth); often used interchangeably with antisocial personality.

client-centered therapy - a nondirective psychotherapy developed by Carl Rogers focusing on empathic understanding, warmth, genuineness, acceptance and unconditional positive regard.

collusion - term referring to the secret, covert "contract" between spouse and offender that allows incestuous abuse to continue in family.

cunnilingus - sexual act where the person derives and stimulates, excitation by licking the clitoris and vulva.

Borderline Personality Disorder - personality disorder in which there is disturbance of mood and interpersonal relations; marked by impulsivity, mood shifts, unpredictability, instability and so forth; often associated with narcissism and antisocial behavior.

decompensation - collapse of the defensive structure resulting in psychotic patterns of thought and behaviors.

denial - defense mechanism operating at preconscious and conscious levels whereby acts, thoughts and feelings are denied; considered a primitive defense similar to repression which operates at the unconscious level.

displacement - defense mechanism whereby energy is rechannelled from one object or person to another. For example, a man is angry with his wife but yells at his children to release the anger.

dissociation - state of separation from behaviors, feelings or thoughts; suggestive of two or more separate personalities emitted by one person as in multiple personalities, fugue states and amnesia.

double bind - a conflict in which avoidance is impossible, often precipitated by contradictory messages from the sender. For example, a mother verbally expresses love while nonverbally rejecting her child.

ego dystonic (ego alien) - term referring to material that is acceptable to an individual in terms of social approval or the image of oneself; opposite of ego syntonic.

ego syntonic - term referring to material that is unacceptable to an individual in terms of social approval or the image of oneself; opposite of ego dystonic.

encopresis - lack of bowel control or soiling; psychogenic or physical in origin; a common symptom of child sexual abuse.

enmeshment - term referring to the interdependent, closed, collusive, secret structure characteristic of incestuous families.

enuresis - lack of bladder control; psychogenic or physical in origin; a common symptom of child sexual abuse.

eroticized anger - phrase referring to the fusion of eroticism and anger; motivator for acts of violence such as sexual assault or rape.

exhibitionism - act of deriving sexual gratification from undressing and/or displaying the genitals.

externalization - see projection

extrafamilial molestation - pedophilic acts occurring outside the family.

fellatio - act of sucking the penis for (mutual) sexual excitation.

fixation - arrest in personality development prior to maturity; may refer to psychosexual stage such as oral or anal fixation; also used to describe fixated child lovers (pedophiles) with exclusive sexual orientation toward children.

functional - relating to psychogenic disorders for which there is no known cure.

Gestalt - type of psychotherapy developed by Fritz Perls emphasizing immediacy of experience, here-and-now, and specific techniques to deal with the influence of past experiences.

homophobia - fear of one's own sex; sometimes a defense against homosexuality.

hysterical personality - personality disorder characterized by emotional instability, overreaction, egocentricity, dependence and attention-seeking behaviors.

identification with the aggressor - phenomenon that often occurs in molestation victims, particularly boys who later perpetrate sex offenses following unconscious identification with the person who abused them.

intrafamilial molestation - incestuous abuse (i.e., abuse occurring within the family).

kleptomania - a compulsion to steal, usually without economic motive; unlike occasional or periodic shoplifting which is a common symptom of child sexual abuse.

"learned helplessness" - phrase associated with Battered Women's Syndrome. Women who are physically and psychologically abused over time internalize blame and experience diminished self-esteem and self-confidence resulting in loss of autonomy and self-determination, dependency and an inability to control their lives.

masochism - submission to psychic or physical pain (often sexual) from another person; opposite of sadism.

Multiple Personality Disorder - condition whereby two or more distinct personalities exist within a single individual. Each personality is fully integrated with unique behaviors, thoughts, memories and so forth.

paraphilia - disorder whereby unusual or bizarre images or acts elicit sexual excitation. Paraphilias include fetishism, pedophilia, exhibitionism, voyeurism and sexual sado-masochism.

pedophilia - disorder whereby preferred or exclusive sexual gratification is obtained with children; homosexual or heterosexual; fixated.

polymorphous perversity - ability to obtain sexual gratification by homosexual, heterosexual and inanimate stimuli of various body zones; characteristic of human infant.

Post Traumatic Stress Disorder (PTSD) - syndrome following traumatic event; symptoms include reliving the event, psychological numbness, recurrent dreams or nightmares, memory impairment, startle response, insomnia.

projection - defense mechanism whereby impulses, feelings, thoughts and behaviors are externalized and attributed to another person. Instead of (unconsciously) "I hate him," the person says, "He hates me."

pseudo incestuous - term used for psychological or emotional seduction through role reversals, inappropriate verbal interactions (sexual innuendos); can be as damaging to victims as overt incestuous abuse.

re-enactment of trauma - act of (unconsciously) reliving unresolved trauma in (unsuccessful) hope of mastery; common symptom in both perpetrators and victims of sex crimes.

reframing - cognitive therapeutic technique involving altering negative self-messages into positive ones. For example, "I can't do it," becomes, "I can try and maybe I will succeed."

regression - phenomenon of reverting to childhood fixations as in dreams and recreation; becomes a pathological defense in sex deviations and character armoring. During stress, the person reverts to childhood fixation points with resultant inability to function on a mature level in certain spheres of life.

sadism - commission of acts involving the infliction of psychic or physical pain on others (often sexual); opposite of masochism.

secondary victimization - phrase referring to psychological damage approaching, equalling, and sometimes, surpassing, that resulting from abuse. This damage is caused by nonsupportive parents, the criminal justice system and so forth.

sequelae - symptoms that occur following remission of, or recovery from, trauma or acute pathology.

sexual misuse - lower end of continuum of abuse involving "minor" transgressions such as inappropriate hugs, verbal innuendos, suggestive looks or stares; often involves precursors to chargeable criminal offenses.

schizophrenia - a large group of disorders with primary and secondary symptoms; characterized by thought disturbance; symptoms include autism, delusions, hallucinations, regression, withdrawal, flattened affect, emotional liability, inappropriate affect, dissocialization and so forth.

status offense - offense that would be criminal if perpetrated by an adult; includes truancy, runaway, curfew violation, etc.

symbiosis - concept borrowed from biology referring to mutual benefits shared in interdependent relationships. Newborns and mothers share symbiotic relationships which become dysfunctional (pathologic) when the children fail to develop autonomy.

symptom substitution or shift - removal of symptom in therapy with replacement by another symptom, sometimes more damaging than the original one.

syndrome - a group or cluster of symptoms representing a particular disorder.

voyeurism - act of deriving sexual gratification by "peeping" or watching others, usually as they undress, shower, masturbate or engage in sexual contact.

Bibliography

Abel, G.G.; Roleau, J and Cunningham-Rathner, J. "Sexually Aggressive Behavior," In (Eds.): Curran, W.; McGarry, A.L.; and Shah, S.A. *Modern Legal Psychiatry and Psychology*. Philadelphia: F.A. Davis Co., 1987.

Abel, G.G.; Mittelman, M.S.; Becker, J.V.; Cunningham-Rathner, J.; and Lucas, L. *The Characteristics of Men Who Molest Young Children*. *Presented at the World Conference on Behavior Therapy*. Washington, D.C., December 10, 1983.

Adler, F., *Sisters in Crime*. N.Y.: McGraw-Hill, 1975.

Amir, M. *Patterns in Forcible Rape*. Chicago: University of Chicago Press, 1971.

Backhouse, C. and Cohen, L. *Sexual Harassment on the Job*. Englewood Cliffs, N.J.: Prentice-Hall, Inc., 1981.

Bernard, G.W.; Robbins, L. et al. "Differences Found Between Rapists and Child Molesters," *Psychological News*, January, 1985.

Briere, J.; Evans, D.; Runtz, M. and Wall, T. "Symptomology in Men Who Were Molested As Children: A Comparative Study," *American Journal of Orthopsychiatry*, Vol. 58, # 3, January 1988, 457-61.

Briere, J. and Runtz, M. "Post Sexual Abuse Trauma: Data and Implications for Clinical Practice," *Journal of Interpersonal Violence*, Vol. II, # 4, December 1987, 367-80.

Brodsky, S.L.; Klemack, S.H.; Skinner, L.J.; Bender, L.Z.; and Polyson, A.M.K. *Sexual Assault: A Literature Analysis and Annotated Bibliography*. National Center for the Prevention and Control of Rape, NIMH, 1977.

Brown, M.E.; Hull, L.A.; and Panesis, S.K. *Women Who Rape.* Boston, MA: Massachusetts Trial Court Office of the Commissioner of Probation, October 12, 1984.

Carmen, E.; Reiker, P.P.; and Mills, T. "Victims of Violence and Psychiatric Illness," *American Journal of Psychiatry*, 141, 1984, 378-83.

Chappell, D.; Geis, R.; and Geis, G. (Eds.). *Forcible Rape: The Crime, The Victim and the Offenders.* N.Y.: Columbia University Press, 1977.

Clark, M. and Grier, P.E. *Female Sexual Offenders in a Prison Setting.* St. Louis, MO.: Behavioral Science Institute, Inc., 1987.

Conoy, S.R.; Templer, D.I.; Brown, R. and Veaco, L. "Parameters of Sexual Contact of Boys With Women," *Archives of Sexual Behavior* 16,5, 1987, 379-95.

Davis, G.E. and Leitenberg, H. "Adolescent Sex Offenders" *Psychological Bulletin*, Vol. 101, 1987, 417-27.

Dean, K.S. and Woods, S.C. *Sexual Abuse of Males Research Project*, Presentation to the Southeastern Regional Conference of Child Welfare League of America, Gatlinburg, TN: May 1985.

De Francis, V. *Protecting the Child Victim of Sex Crimes Committed by Adults.* Denver, CO: American Humane Association, 1969.

de River, J.P. *The Sexual Criminal: A Psychoanalytical Study.* Springfield, IL: Charles C. Thomas, 1950.

Faller, K. "Women Who Sexually Abuse Children," *Violence and Victims*, 2, 4, 1987, 263-76.

Family Sexual Abuse Project of the Saint Paul Foundation. "Another Secret Out In the Open: Female Sex Offenders" and, "Profile of Female Sex Offenders and Treatment Effectiveness Is Focus of Genesis II Study," *Looking Ahead*, 1, 1, St. Paul, MN. Spring 1987.

Fehrenbach, P.A. et al. "Adolescent Sex Offenders: Gender and Offense Characteristics," *American Journal of Orthopsychiatry*, 56, 225-33.

Feyerherm, W.H. and Pope, C. *Gender Bias in Juvenile Court Disposition*, Presented at the Annual Meeting of the Western Society of Criminology, 1980.

Feyerherm, W. "Measuring Gender Differences in Delinquency: Self Reports Versus Police Contact," In (Ed.): Warren, M.Q. *Comparing Female and Male Offenders*. Beverly Hills, CA: Sage Publications 1981.

Figueira-McDonough, J.; Barton, W.H.; and Sarri, R.C. "Normal Deviance: Gender Similarities in Adolescent Subcultures," In (Ed): Warren, M.Q. *Comparing Female and Male Offenders*. Beverly Hills, CA: Sage Publications, 1981.

Finkelhor, D. *Child Sexual Abuse*. N.Y.: The Free Press, 1984.

Finkelhor, D. and Russell, D. "Women As Perpetrators: Review of the Evidence," In (Ed.): Finkelhor, D. *Child Sexual Abuse: New Theory and Research*. N.Y. The Free Press, 1984, 171-87.

Finkelhor, D. et al. A Sourcebook on Child Sexual Abuse. Beverly Hills, CA: Sage Publications, 1986.

Finkelhor, D. and Williams, L.M. *Nursery Crimes*. Beverly Hills: Sage Publications, 1988.

Forward, S and Buck, C. *Betrayal of Innocence: Incest and its Devastation*. N.Y. Penguin, 1979.

Genesis II For Women, Inc. *Genesis II Female Sex Offender Programming*, Minneapolis, MIN, 1987.

Groth, A.N. *Men Who Rape: The Psychology of the Offender*. N.Y.: Plenum, 1981 (1979).

Groth, A.N. *Men Raped by Women*, San Francisco Chronicle, March 15, 1982.

Haugaard, J.J. and Reppucci, N.D. *The Sexual Abuse of Children: A Comprehensive Guide to Current Knowledge and Intervention Strategies*. San Francisco, CA: Jossey-Bass, Inc., Publisher, 1988.

Herman, J. *Father-Daughter Incest*. Cambridge, MA: Harvard University Press, 1981.

Jackson, M. *PHASE Extends to Female Sex Abusers*, Ramsey County Review, Ramsey County, MN, September 5, 1986.

Johns, R.L. and Shier, D. K. *Sexual Molestation of Boys by Females*, American Psychological Association Annual Meeting, Dallas, TX, May 22, 1985.

Justice, B. and Justice, R. *The Broken Taboo: Sex in the Family*. N.Y.: Human Sciences Press, 1979, 193-95.

Johnson, R.L. and Shrier, D. "Past Sexual Victimization by Females of Male Patients in an Adolescent Medicine, Clinical Population," *Journal of Psychiatry*, 144, 5, 1987, 650-52.

Kaslow, F.; Haupt, D.; Arce, A.A.; and Werblowsky, J. "Homosexual Incest," *Psychiatric Quarterly*, 53, 1981, 184-93.

Kappel, S. *Adolescent Sex Offenders in Vermont*, Burlington, VT: Vermont Department of Health, 1985.

Knopp, F.H. and Lackey, L.B.. *Female Sexual Abusers: A Summary of Data from 44 Treatment Providers*, Orwell, VT: Safer Society Program, 1987.

Knopp, F.H.; Rosenberg, J.; and Stevenson, W. *Report on Nationwide Survey of Juvenile and Adult Sex Offender Treatment Programs and Providers*, Orwell, VT: Safer Society Press, 1986.

Lew, M. *Victims No Longer: Men Recovering From Incest and Other Sexual Child Abuse.* N.Y.: Nevraumont Publishing Company., 1988.

Marvasti, J. "Incestuous Mothers," *American Journal of Forensic Psychiatry*, 7,4. 1986, 63-69.

Mathews, R. *Female Sexual Offenders,* Notes from a Workshop Presented to the Third National Adolescent Perpetrator Network Meeting, Keystone, CO. May 1987.

Mathews, R.; Mathews, J.K.; and Speltz, K. *Female Sexual Offenders: An Exploratory Study,* Orwell, VT: The Safer Society Press, 1989.

Mathews, R. "Female Sexual Offenders: Treatment and Legal Issues," *PHASE and Genesis II for Women,* Minneapolis, MN, 1987.

Mathews, R. "Preliminary Typology of Female Sex Offenders," *PHASE and Genesis II for Women,* Minneapolis, MN: 1987.

Mathews, R. *PHASE Female Sexual Offender Case Construction: Important Question Areas,* Maplewood, MN: East Communities Family Center, 1987.

Meiselman, K. Incest: A Psychological Study of Causes and Effects With Treatment Recommendations, San Francisco, CA: Jossey-Bass, 1978.

McCarty, L.M. "Mother-Child Incest: Characteristics of the Offender," *Child Welfare*, 65,5,1986, 447-58.

McCarty, L.M. *Women and Rape,* Presented at the Third Annual Convention on the Evaluation and Treatment of Sexual Aggressives, Avila Beach, CA, March 1981.

MacDonald, A.P. "Same-Sex Incest: the Too Too Taboo," *Journal of Sex Education and Therapy,* Vol. 12, #1, Summer, 1986, 18-20.

Money, J. and Schwartz, M. "Biosocial Determinates of Gender Identity Differentiation and Development," In (Ed.): Hutchinson, J.B. *Biological Determinates of Sexual Behavior*, N.Y.: Wiley, 1978.

O'Connor, A.A. "Female Sex Offenders," *British Journal of Psychiatry*, 150, 1987, 615-20.

"PHASE Adolescent Female Sex-Offender Education, Assessment and Treatment Program," Maplewood, MN, 1987.

Petrovich, M. and Templer, D.I. "Heterosexual Molestation of Children Who Later Become Rapists," *Psychological Reports*, 54, 810, 1984.

Pollack, O. *The Criminality of Women*. N.Y.: Penguin, 1961.

"Preliminary Report From the National Task Force on Juvenile Sexual Offenders," Juvenile and Family Court Journal, Vol. 39, #2, 1988.

Reckless, W. and Kay, B. *The Female Offenders*. Washington, D.C.: President's Commission on Law Enforcement and Administration of Justice, 1967.

Russell, D.E.H. (Ed.) *Sexual Exploitation: Rape, Child Sexual Abuse, and Workplace Harassment*. Beverly HIlls, CA: Safe Publications, 1984.

Russell, D.E.H. *The Secret Trauma: Incest in the Lives of Girls and Women*. N.Y.: Basic Books, 1986.

Russell, D.E.H. and Finkelhor, D. "The Gender Gap Among Perpetrators of Child Sexual Abuse," In (Ed.): Russell, D.E.H. *Sexual Exploitation: Rape, Child Sexual Abuse, and Workplace Harassment*. Beverly Hills, CA: Sage Publications, 1984.

Sarrell, P.M. and Masters, W.H. "Sexual Molestation of Men By Women," *Archives of Sexual Behavior*, 11,2, 1982, 117-31.

Schlesinger, L.J. & Revitch, E. (Eds.) *Sexual Dynamics of Anti-Social Behavior*. Springfield, IL: Charles C. Thomas, 1983.

Sgroi, S. (Ed.) *Handbook of Clinical Intervention in Child Sexual Abuse*. Lexington, MA: D.C. Heath and Company, 1982, 39-79.

Timnick, L. "When Women Rape Men," *Psychology Today*, September, 1983, 74.

U.S. Dept. of Justice. *Uniform Crime Reports for the U.S.*, 1975-78, Washington, D.C.: Government Printing Office, October 12, 1984.

Wahl, C.W. "The Psychodynamics of Consumated Maternal Incest," *Archives of General Psychiatry*, August, 1960, 188-93.

Walters, D.R. *Physical and Sexual Abuse of Children: Causes and Treatment*. Bloomington, IN: Indiana University Press, 1975, 122.

Warren, M.Q. (Ed.). *Comparing Female and Male Offenders*. Beverly Hills, CA: Sage Publications, 1981.

Warren, M.Q. (Ed.) "Gender Comparisons in Crime and Delinquency," In (Ed.): Warren, M.Q. *Comparing Female and Male Offenders*. Beverly Hills, CA: Sage Publications, 1981.

Webster, D.C. and Masters, R.E.L. (Eds.) *Violation of Taboo: Incest in the Great Literature of the Past and the Present*. N.Y.: The Julian Press, 1963.

Wolfe, F.A. *Twelve Female Sexual Offenders*, Presentation to "Next Steps in Research on the Assessment and Treatment of Sexually Aggressive Persons (Paraphiliacs)," St. Louis, MO, March, 1985.

INDEX